MAKING CARS

Sandy
Transport
Society 172.

History Workshop Series

General Editor
Raphael Samuel, *Ruskin College, Oxford*

MAKING CARS

A history of car making in Cowley...
...by the people who make the cars

Television History Workshop

Editors
Greg Lanning, Christine Peaker, Caro Webb, Richard White

Research and Interviews
Christine Peaker, Caro Webb, Richard White

with Bill Bourne, Dee Bourne, Adam Ganz, Viviane Hurley, Ruth Richardson, Bridget Sneyd and Steve Tolliday

Routledge & Kegan Paul
London, Boston and Henley

First published in 1985 LB
by Routledge & Kegan Paul plc

14 Leicester Square, London WC2H 7PH, England

9 Park Street, Boston, Mass. 02108, USA

Broadway House, Newtown Road,
Henley-on-Thames, Oxon RG9 1EN, England

Set in Bembo, 11 on 12 pt
by Input Typesetting Ltd, London
and printed in Great Britain
by The Thetford Press Ltd
Thetford, Norfolk

© Television History Centre 1985

Library of Congress Cataloging in Publication Data

Main entry under title:
Making cars.
(History workshop series)
Includes index.
1. Automobile industry workers—England—Oxford—
History.   2. Automobile industry and trade—England—
Oxford—History.   3. Cowley (Oxford, Eng.)   I. Peaker,
Christine.   II. Webb, Caro.   III. White, Richard.
IV. Lanning, Greg.   V. Television History Workshop
(Great Britain)   VI. Series.
HD8039.A82G75   1985   338.4'76292'0942574   84–13398

British Library CIP Data also available.

ISBN 0–7102–0272–5

PEOPLE MAKE CARS

'There is no stereotype car worker—they're a cross section of society with all abilities, all aims, all ambitions, all aspirations, but they're all in there doing a common job and they're all subservient to the manufacturing process, and it's this desire to individualise yourself and express yourself whilst you're at work is what it's all about, in my view.'

PETER DAVIS,
Pressed Steel 1960-80

Contents

Introduction

This is the story of car making at the Morris Motors and Pressed Steel Fisher factories at Cowley, Oxford. Thousands of men and women have been using their skills and energies to make cars. They have had to learn new skills and new ways of working and then adapt to further changes. They have struggled to organise and maintain their trade unions. The management have introduced changes and themselves been changed. All know intimately the satisfactions and dissatisfactions involved in MAKING CARS. This is their history.

The Industry

The car manufacturing industry is central to the British economy. This history is therefore also the inside story of the workings of the British economy over the last seventy years. The progress of Morris Motors from small-scale production, through labour-intensive mass production, to the current high levels of automation, mirrors the transformation of the work process throughout British industry. The company, founded by a capitalist entrepreneur, William Morris, grew by swallowing many of its competitors and suppliers, before merging with its chief British rival, Austin Motors, to create the British Motor Company in 1952. It was hoped that BMC would be large enough to compete with the giant American car companies Ford and General Motors. In 1968 the government encouraged BMC to merge with Leyland Motors in search of greater scale and efficiency. British Leyland introduced a new corporate structure and new management systems in line with current theories of business management. This did not prevent the company from going bankrupt in 1974. The government provided huge sums of state aid to enable BL to survive into the 1980s.

Today

At Cowley, 12,000 people make 4,000 cars every week. Every two minutes of the working day a car comes off the production line. In 1983 the factories were making the Triumph Acclaim, the Ambassador, the Rover Saloon and the recently introduced Maestro. This is the latest in a long series of famous cars that have come from Cowley, including the Bullnose Morris, the Morris Minor and the Mini.

There are two factories at Cowley: Morris Motors and Pressed Steel, both part of BL Cars Ltd. Pressed Steel is the body plant, which presses out the sheet steel into the various shapes that go to make up a car body. Across the road is the Morris Motors Assembly plant, where the engines, wheels, seats, and interior trim are fitted. Although the two factories are next door to each other, their histories are different, and people remember them differently. The two styles of management as well as variations in the work itself have affected the growth of the unions and the lives of the people who worked there.

Images

The advertisements for cars speak of glamour and excitement. The advertisement for the Triumph Acclaim made at Cowley:

'The Triumph Acclaim, the car that's been designed and built to be totally equipped for today's driving. On all roads, in all conditions, in total luxury. The Triumph Acclaim.'

This book is not about the image of the car. It is a history of car making in Cowley, by the people who make the cars. It is about the way cars are made and the way the work has changed over the last seventy years. It is also about making history. We tried to reach as many people as we could who have worked, or are still working, at Cowley, to invite them to help in this history. All the contributors have worked in the same place, but their memories vary and are often contradictory. We have tried to reflect these contradictions.

Official accounts of the economy and the car industry treat the car-makers as an undifferentiated mass. The aim of this history is to reveal and restore the human dimension of Making Cars.

1   *The Early Days – 1910–30*

Beginnings

Cowley has not always been an industrial area. In the early years of this century, it was a small village lying just outside the university town of Oxford. Most of the people living there worked either on the land, or as servants in the Oxford colleges.

'I was born in Headington Quarry which is not far from here, the oldest child of a college labourer . . . I had dreams when I was a child of going to Canada . . . I read all books of Canada and Australia and my idea was to leave England and live abroad, go exploring . . . When you start work all those dreams go for a Burton.

'So I found myself at fourteen and six weeks at Morris Motors in the body shop.'   LG ★

'You see, Cowley was just a straggling village . . . a lot of people used to come in local. It built up over the northside and people was coming from all over.'   CY

'W. R. Morris founded a bicycle repair shop in Oxford in the 1890s, built the first Morris bike in 1894, followed it with motor cycles from 1901 and started to design his first car in 1911. Deliveries began in March 1913. Morris used the old Military Training College in Cowley to house his production lines. During the Great War the old Military College produced munitions alongside the cars. Production in 1920, was 1,932 but by 1925 Morris was turning out over 54,000 cars a year.' (*BL Heritage Catalogue*)

Memories of William Morris vary. Some of those who have talked with us remember him with admiration. But he dominates some memories as he dominated the factory.

★ Contributors' full names are given on p. 126.

6

W. R. Morris

1919...

MORRIS OXFORD CARS.

Harry Kerry started at Morris's in 1919 and worked as a transport driver, taking the chassis from one part of the factory to another. He took these photographs of his fellow drivers during their lunch break one day.

This picture shows Harry Kerry on the chassis of one of the early Bullnose Oxfords.

'That's a chassis we used to have like that for towing...all our brakes were rod brakes...there was no front brake at all...and we used to stand one foot on the chassis, one foot on the brake. That's how we used to tow them and we used to keep going in rain, hail or snow...'

'This picture was taken when there was no buildings at the bottom of the works at all, that was all open ground.'

1923...

*Ellen Bateman started at the factory in 1915. She began working on
shell-cases for the First World War, and then she started on cars.*

'I was about seventeen or eighteen then and there was just the
three of us and we used to do the springs of the car. Grease and
cover them with gaiters.

'Three of us lived in this old cubby hole at the end of the tall
building where Lord Nuffield [William Morris] used to live
and it was a very small place. There was a long place as you
know where the men were working. We didn't even have a
chair to sit on. It was very very poor to start but any rate we
were earning a little bit of money.

'I'd like to tell you a little bit about Mr Morris. They used to
have a whist drive up in that big building, the old place, and
he and his wife always used to come. I remember one whist
drive I had a prize and that was a box of a dozen boxes of
matches in it. I thought that was a marvellous prize, after the
war and all that sort of thing. Another thing he did for his
staff, he used to give us a chicken every year. Then it went on
that he hired the town hall at Oxford and gave us a marvellous
do there.' EB

'The Bullnose Oxford and the Cowley was made in two different
departments. We used to feed the Oxfords in the bottom end
and go round and go in again and feed the Cowley in the next
block of flats.

'This is the chassis we used to have for towing – feeding the
blocks, and they used to go over a bridge into Mrs Bateman's
husband's department for wiring to do their stuff and that's
where we towers picked the chassis up, three lengths of rope.

'I shall always remember Joe Hardy's man, old Fred with his
horse and trolley, who used to collect the ashes. The horse
used to make muck on the roads, you know, do his business on
the road – of course there was no wings on our vehicles, they
were just plain wheels, and well, we poor blokes, all the muck
and wet used to come up all over us if we never spotted this
muck. Anyway old Billy thought about it and made
arrangements for this poor old Fred, so as soon as the horse
wanted to do his business he had to grab a bucket and hold and
catch it and if he missed any he'd got to get out and clean it
up. That was one bit of fun we used to have.' HK

Morris Motors in the Twenties

Morris Motors pioneered cheaper mass-produced cars in England. In the 1920s Morris Motors' prosperity was built around two cars, the Oxford and the Cowley, which were produced on a mass production basis with continued price cutting. The Oxford cost £590 in 1921 but only £260 in 1925. The number of employees shot up from 200 in 1919 to over 5,000 in 1925. In the same period, production of cars jumped from just 216 in 1919 to 55,582 in 1925. Pre-tax profits rose from £1,500 in 1919 to £1,556,000 in 1925.

The dramatic growth of Morris Motors was partly based on the introduction of simple mass production techniques at the Cowley factory. Cars were assembled on production lines, and the work was broken down into repetitive tasks which could be performed rapidly. The chassis was towed from building to building and then pushed down the production line. Each worker or gang of workers had their own job and were no longer responsible for producing a whole car but merely completing part of the assembly. In this way, with workers being paid for each completed task, cars could be produced faster and management could calculate costs more accurately.

Morris's success was also based on the use of outside suppliers. By offering them guaranteed long runs Morris kept their prices low whilst not devoting any of Morris's capital to installing equipment and training operators to make the different parts.

'For the "Bullnose" and many subsequent models the Morris factory merely assembled the cars – e.g. engines and gearboxes came from White and Poppe, axles and steering from E. G. Wrigley, bodies from local coach builders, Raworths, and wheels from Sanky.' (*BL Heritage Catalogue*)

Mass Production

Making cars in the early 1920s was a lengthy business. There was no moving line, so cars were pushed from one area to the next. The body was made from wood, using the old coach-building techniques. The chassis was assembled separately. The engine was bolted into position and the wheels put on. The body was then lowered onto the chassis and finally the seats and interior were fitted.

In 1972, Dave Lyddon began work at Cowley. He has been researching into the ways in which car production has changed.

'Mass production started up in the early twenties, and Morris

was one of the first factories. It's not like we understand it today, although there were line systems for parts of production on many of them – for instance, the bodies that Morris's were still building were still made of wood. So you had the sawmill, which was a very large building, machining wood to exact specifications which would then be fitted together on standing trestles. You notice if you look at the men making them, they're wearing white aprons, ties, waistcoats and so on, it's a standard sort of dress for that type of work. It was fairly clean work but wood shaving everywhere because the pieces never fitted exactly. It was more of a fitting job rather than an assembly job as we get today.'   DL

George Weekes started at Morris's in 1924.

'When you worked on the job there was no guides or anything down, no chains . . . as you did a car, probably four of you working on a car, you pushed the cars up, walked back a bit and pushed the car up again.'   GW

Monty Hillier started work at Morris's as a boy of fifteen.

'The particular job I did was putting door pads on – fourteen or fifteen years old each and you had to put these door pads on. They gave you a pump screwdriver, and a garnisher which we called the bradle. I think that's all we needed. In those days people wore aprons, we kept our screws in the top, bent over the door to put the screw in, pumped it and holding your leg against the door. Of course there was no toilet time allowed, so what you did was the other three boys would carry on if you went out the back. You did five or six cars up the line because the lines didn't move then.

We had a good old charge hand and he called you cock, "Come on, my cocks", and he used to hit you with a little stick, joking – he was a nice man actually, "Come on, my cocks," and he'd always say "Up the line or up the office," so you had to get a move on.'   MH

Publicity

The Film At Cowley was made in the 1920s to explain the car-making process. It was made for publicity. This is the commentary.

Monty Gibbs started at Morris in 1922. Unlike most Morris workers, he had regular employment at the factory so he was able to save up and buy a second-hand Bullnose Morris.

'This is me and my Bullnose Morris. That Bullnose Morris I had for about five years I think, it cost me—I think it cost £60 when I bought it. And that's the Bullnose. I kept it about four or five years, it never went wrong but it was a bounder for punctures. We went to Southsea, we had about five punctures.'

MONTY GIBBS,
Morris Motors 1922-70

'It is a marvellous scene of beautifully organised industrial activity. There is no sense of rush or bustle. Every man seems to have plenty of time to do what he has to do. There is nothing skimped and as a result the quality turned out is extraordinarily good. As an example of well-timed sequences and dovetailing operations it is most impressive. Yet although they are working hard, they never give one the impression they are over-worked, and there is an atmosphere of happy contentment in all Morris shops, which is really extraordinarily pleasant to see.'

The Sawmill

Morris's had a sawmill in the 1920s where parts for the wooden car bodies were produced. Mr Fred Thornton told us that he suffered congestion of the lungs from exposure to the sawdust there. He was transferred to a cleaner job by a sports-loving manager, who wanted him for the cricket team.

The Foundry

In the early 1920s, Morris Motors had its own foundry, where some car parts were moulded and cast.

'I done all the jobs in the foundry . . . it was terrible, you couldn't see your hand before you. I was so sooted up nothing could get it away . . . if you walked up and down there once and came back you'd have to change all your clothes . . . We had sand, we had soot and treacle, we had loads of manure all going into the mixer to make the moulds, you see, and when that was all mixed up it was like cement.'   GP

Radiators

Arthur Exell began at Cowley in 1929.

'You'd be surprised, I was very proud because you could look over there and we'd say, "I made that radiator," "rad" we used to call it. "I made that rad," and honestly we had to put our

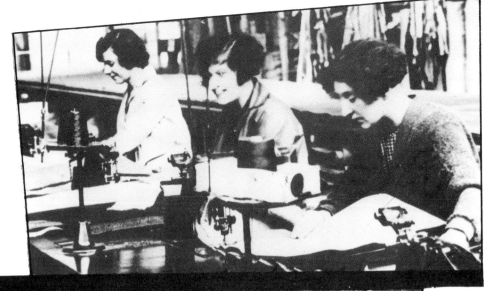

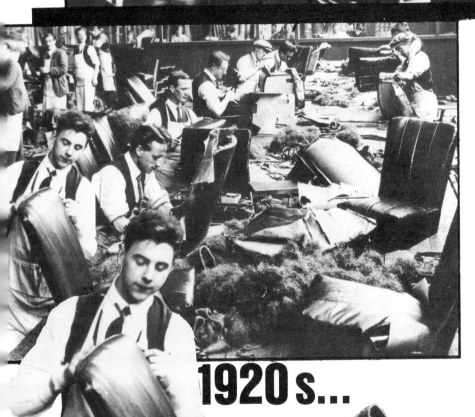

1920 s...

name on the top of the radiator, which had a felting round. You lifted the felting and scribbled your name on. And years afterwards we had radiators come back for repairs and we've had a look at them: "That's mine, I done that one." Things like that you see and you are very proud of the fact. Because the radiator was a good thing to make, enjoyable the work was doing it.'   AE

Trim Shop

'Now you turn to the trim shop, you see here [p. 15] female sewing machinists, and yet the people making up the seats are men, and they're building seats using horse hair, probably leather or – or a leather substitute material. Using – just ordinary trimmer's hammer and tacks, working fairly close together but no notion of mass production or line systems and that's really what characterises the twenties.'   DL

Images

'If you watch the young ladies whose mission in life it is to sew pleats into the upholstery material you will see that she works with uncanny accuracy but when she has made the pleats they are filled with stuffing in a most ingenious manner. A big tube used as a needle pushing the stuffing through the pleats in which it is retained on the return stroke. Harder work such as this of course done by boys or young men and not by women. Everywhere properly graded labour is arranged in the Morris works and all the way up the workbenches you see evidence of the cheerful spirit and the keen way in which all these Morris operators handle all their work.' (*BMC Film At Cowley*)

Morris Motors in 1930

The Morris Minor was introduced in 1929 and sold in its cheapest version for £125. After Pressed Steel was established the introduction of the steel body helped production reach 58,436 cars in 1930. The number of employees in the whole company rose to 10,000. Profits were £1,527,000.

'Cowley was a big and busy place in 1926, but almost puny compared with its size today. The housing problem for cars at Cowley is just as pressing as for the works. Building of houses goes on apace all round, the car habitations cover some 86 acres. The workers, some 5,000 of them at Cowley, flow in and out of the works at their appointed hours; the cars flow out only – always moving – an orderly but irresistible torrent.' (*Autocar* Magazine, 1929)

Pressed Steel Begins

'The firm began to expand. We were moved to the far end of the works . . . We had a very good outlook there. We could look out of our main doors and see all the nice green fields. Until one day the bulldozers came along . . . They weren't bulldozers in those days, they were two traction engines, one each side of the field . . . and anyway instead of seeing the nice green fields around all we could see was Pressed Steel suddenly start up.' MG

'The Pressed Steel Company of Great Britain Ltd. began in 1926 when William Morris persuaded the Edward G. Budd Manufacturing Company of Philadelphia USA and the merchant bankers J. Henry Schroder and Co. to join him in establishing the Pressed Steel Company next door to Morris's own Cowley factory.' (*Pressed Steel Shareholders' Report, 1958.*)

In 1926, the Pressed Steel factory was built beside the Morris works. It brought large-scale heavy industry to a predominantly rural area. Initially, Pressed Steel produced car bodies just for Morris Motors, but within a few years it became a fully independent company producing car bodies for motor manufacturers and later produced other metal items such as fridges.

Pressed Steel brought new technology from the Detroit car industry. It was now possible to produce all-steel car bodies and move away from wooden construction. Pressed Steel supplied several car companies.

Alec Robinson was one of the first workers at Pressed Steel. He started in 1927 and worked there until 1970.

'This is the first time these things had ever arrived in Britain. There was nothing like this before. They were giants. They were enormous things. You just caught hold of the great big sheet of steel, perhaps two on one side, two the other, and slid it into position. Then you pulled the lever and down came the top die. The bottom die came up as well and then you got the complete shape of the two dies, the male and female dies. Sometimes it was a back panel or a side panel or great big chassis member, something of the sort. All sorts of things.' AR

Haydn Evans was a trip hammer operator for many years and is now afflicted with tinnitus – a constant ringing in his ears.

'My first impression going round the factory were, it was bedlam, absolute bedlam. The machine that I was operating was the loudest ever created.

'Our job was to take parts of a motor car in the raw stage steel, and when they came out from the press shop perhaps they hadn't been perfectly formed, they were corrugated, and our job then was to use this trip hammer, which was two dies beating the metal. We'd work the metal in between the dies operating it and flatten out all the corrugations and reshape. It was marvellous, you could actually reshape parts of metal with this machine. But it was a terrible din. You had to watch that you held the thing, you know, really right. If you had it lopsided you could cut your hand off. Anyway the first time I put my foot on the treadle of this hammer and brrr, it frightened me to death.' HE

'I'll give an indication of the kind of conditions we had to work in. You were on a conveyor – it was the start of the whole metal body that was being produced after Nuffield had been to America and seen how they produced metal bodies, and the Morris 8 was one of the first ones ever produced in this country done on a conveyor. On the side panel line you had about six foot to work in. You had to manoeuvre a quarter-ton transformer in that six foot and carry out the operations of doing your welding around the top where the door fits and the rear window. Then jump out from under the panel, pick up a big punch and punch in some holes in the bottom of the panel in order to get it on the jig and the next stage of the operation. After about three months I went home. It was probably about Easter. I frightened my mother to death. She looked at me and thought I had galloping consumption which was prevalent in those days. I'd gone down from about 13 stone to 9 stone 3! It put the fear of God up her!' NB

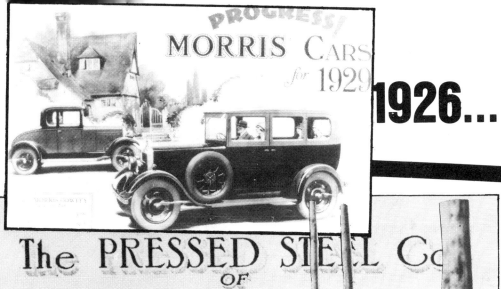

MORRIS CARS for 1929

PROGRESS!

1926...

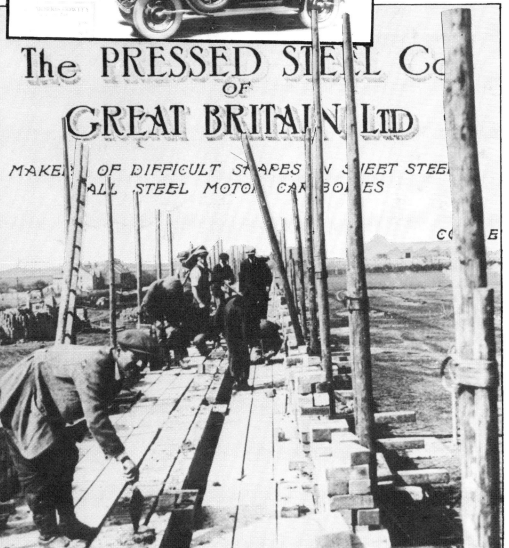

The PRESSED STEEL Co
OF
GREAT BRITAIN LTD

MAKERS OF DIFFICULT SHAPES IN SHEET STEEL
ALL STEEL MOTOR CAR BODIES

Morris Motors and the Car Industry 1910–1930

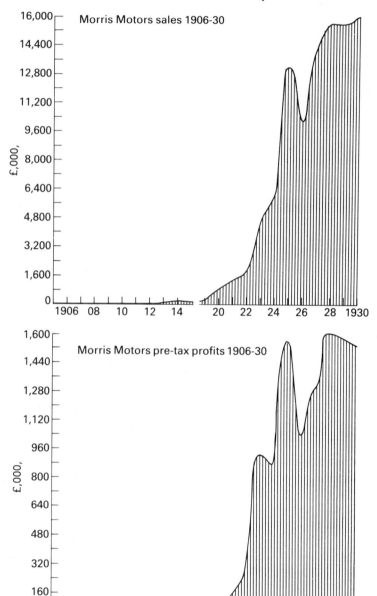

Morris Motors sales 1906-30

Morris Motors pre-tax profits 1906-30

WORKING FOR THE GOVERNMENT Morris made profits of £23,500 in 1916, £16,200 in 1917, £18,900 in 1918. Some cars were produced though: 907 in 1914, 320 in 1915, 697 in 1916, 126 in 1917.

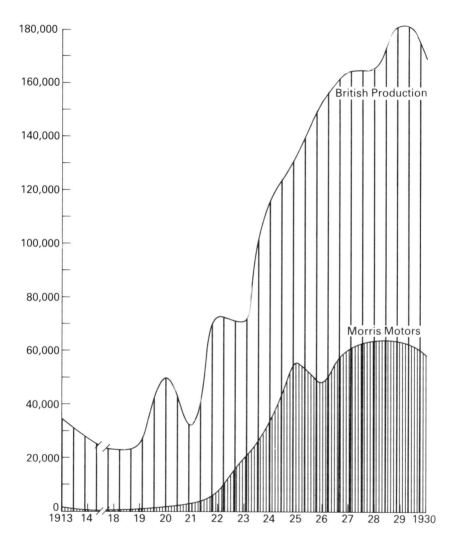

Car production at Morris Motors
and total British Car production

In 1920 there were over 200 car manufacturers but the US-owned Ford company produced
40,000 out of the 50,000 cars produced that year. Morris produced just under 2,000 cars.
By 1930 Morris was producing around one-third of all cars made in Britain

Percy Fray started work there in 1927.

'You used to wear anything, old rags or waste, because mostly it was waist high you was working. And you'd be thick with grease. So when you take your waistcoat off (them days we'd wear a waistcoat and a shirt) you could scrape it off your tummy like butter – you didn't worry about that though.'   PF

'It wasn't till I was married that I really realised what conditions he went through with the clothes and things. Because of course his landlady used to do his washing till I got married to him. I used to have to soak his shirt in paraffin before you could wash it, to get all this grease off. And they also used to burn their clothes a lot even with the riveting.'   AF

2 The Thirties and Forties

The Search for Work

New workers at the factory travelled long distances, and the sight of hundreds of men bicycling to and from the works at Cowley was very common.

'They'd come thirty or forty miles around here to get work. They used to cycle twelve and fourteen miles a day, every day, to come here, from the surrounding villages and places around Oxford. Well, it was the only transport they had in those days, there were no buses in the little villages.' AR

With the onset of the Depression, more workers came from far and wide to find work in the young car industry at Cowley.

'I worked at the Swindon [railway] works as an apprentice and I started work there in 1919 and left in 1926 . . . When I came to start at Pressed Steel I'd been out of work a twelvemonth.' PF

'You see, in those days they didn't have a labour exchange . . . When all these men came up, I think they had to walk from the station to Morris and Pressed Steel. They'd got nowhere to sleep or anything, just came as they were because they wanted a job.' EB

In 1927, Arthur Exell joined a Hunger March from South Wales to London.

'I think it was somewhere in November we left for London. It was a terrible, terrible journey, that's the only thing I can say, because none of us was prepared for anything like that. We were all underfed, very underfed, and we didn't have good boots or anything, so we just continued. It was surprising how many had to drop out, going along the road, they just couldn't keep up with it, their feet was too sore.

'I had my first big shock because one of the men died. It was decided that we would carry this man along with us because we couldn't bury him, but before we got to a little place called Yorkley another one had died. So we were carrying two men along then in our arms, and then when we got to Yorkley and Bream, near Chepstow, we asked from the church could they provide something for us to bury the men. They said yes if you pay and we couldn't pay – we had no money. It was a very very difficult position to be in and in the end we dug out an ordinary grave and put them in and dropped them in the grave and then continued the journey leaving them there.'   AE

Arthur Exell got work in Oxford along the way and a year later started at Morris Radiators. He has written his own account of working there.★

Pressed Steel in the Thirties

Norman Brown was offered work at Pressed Steel in 1935.

'In the thirties in Wigan, there were cotton-mills, and I can remember those being pulled down and all the factory chimneys. It was just desolate and there was no chance of any work for anybody, not in those days.

'I think I had about half a crown when I left home and that had to last me about a fortnight, as you had to work a week in hand. I remember when I got into Oxford, we had to go from the station up to the Cowley factory and all I'd got was my half-crown. There was two or three of us got on the buses, and some old boy, I don't know who he was to this day, paid our fares to Cowley. God bless him, I don't know who he was. That was my first taste of Oxford, being run up on the bus to the Swan and then walking to the factory. You had to walk past Morris's to get to Pressed Steel, and even then I think you could get the kind of feeling of what it was going to be like because as soon as you got near the Pressed Steel factory it just stunk of old oil and all that kind of stuff.'   NB

Haydn Evans arrived at Pressed Steel from South Wales in 1933.

★*The Politics of the Production Line: Autobiography of an Oxford Car Worker*, by Arthur Exell. *A History Workshop Journal* pamphlet, 1981.

1930s...

'Well, I was twenty-three years of age and there was a deep depression at Merthyr, I'd left the collieries – about the collieries, you mentioned as a matter of fact I'd come out suffering with this nystagmus,* but in that eighteen months I was sufficiently cured that I could do the job on the outside, in the outside world. As I had a sister living in Oxford I thought, well, the best place for me was Oxford. There was not much going on in Merthyr town, it was a deep depression, and inasmuch as the car industry was opening up I thought I'd seek fame and fortune and notoriety whatever you call it in Oxford.'
HE

Injuries

Without enough guards and other shop floor safety features characteristic of modern factories, injuries to Pressed Steel workers were common. In 1958 Pressed Steel management looked back with pride at the provision they made for those injured in the factory.

'During this [prewar] period valuable progress was achieved on the welfare side. As early as 1929, life insurance policies were made available to every worker . . . two years later a small hospital was built within the bounds of the factory, fully equipped and staffed with full-time doctors and nurses, a step that was quite unusual at the time.' (*Pressed Steel Shareholders' Report, 1958*)

Haydn Evans was a shop steward at Pressed Steel in the thirties.

'I was working on the trip hammer one day, it's got a terrific beat on it, and my little finger was sticking out while I was running metal across and I run it over the tip of my finger. I went to the inspector at the side. I had cotton gloves on and the end of the glove was smashed. So I said, "I think I've smashed my finger," and I pulled it off.

'It was all splashed out so I went to the hospital and they sent me down the Radcliffe and that was that. Now it's much shorter. I had the thirty shillings for two weeks and then went back to work. I had an interview with the doctor (this is a fact

*Nystagmus is a distressing condition, characterised by persistent uncontrollable movements of the eye, which occurs in coal miners and is caused by working in inadequate light.

that I'm telling you), "Oh," he said, "Mr Evans, how do you do?" and he put his hand out – naturally to shake hands, which was rather peculiar, you know, they don't generally shake hands with anybody who come in, and I shook hands. "Oh," he said, "your grip hasn't been affected at all," he said, "with the loss of your tip of your finger, nothing the matter with you." Well, I wasn't going to claim in any case. At that particular time I didn't think you could. You know, they gave you thirty shillings compensation, £1.50p. today, and that was the end of it.' HE

'One of the first impressions I got when I went in the factory – each stanchion had a first aid kit on it, a stretcher on it – right the way through the press. Loss of fingers, thumbs and hands was commonplace in the factory. I see one bloke had his hand off one day. He'd just turned round to say something to someone who was walking past, and before you could get at him, his hand had gone. The presses they operated were huge things, the size of a house, two-storey house. Presses that came down weighed tons. He didn't even know that his hand had gone. He went to take the next panel – that was it, he never felt it. He was actually a good boxer and they thought he had a chance of making the championship, but he went to hospital and that was it, his hand was off.' NB

We asked Norman Brown if he had ever been injured. He chuckled. 'No, no. I just wore out, that's all.'
Alec Robinson went to Pressed Steel a year after it was built.

'It was very dangerous. You see, what happened, there were people working in there from the farms and from shops and from all walks of life that had never seen this machinery before and they were handling it and they were trying to work as fast and as hard as they can to earn as much so they were taking risks, and of course there was terrible accidents in there. There were several men walking around with their hands off and then in the press shop these great big presses, as I said, they came up from the bottom and down from the top and they rammed the metal and one day a chap had got a panel stuck in there. It was tied up and he couldn't get it out, so the foreman went in there, he got his head up underneath and he was pulling and pulling and down this press came and of course his head was in

there and his head was just like red paint. All over the press
. . . it was terrible.'   AR

'Conditions counted for nothing really. You were willing to
accept the most primitive conditions. In some case where you'd
see a man working on lead, all he had over his head was a piece
of rag he'd brought from home, a little mask of a piece of tin
and a bit of cotton wool. When they came off the job, they
looked a jolly sight dirtier than if they'd been down the coal
mine working at the face and they used to go home in that
condition. The washing facilities were conspicuous by their
absence and safety and conditions were secondary, as far as I'm
concerned, they counted for nothing. All they wanted was to
earn as much money in as quick a time as they could and get
out.'   AC

Lead

'We were working a few yards away from the lead and right
close into the vicinity of the compressed air hammers, and the
noise from those you couldn't hear yourself speak. The lead was
in the air . . . it was really filthy . . . The men were given free
milk . . . they were forced to attend the hospital unit at certain
times in rotation every day . . . for checks on their lead intake
. . . All the weld spots were covered with lead: leadfilling . . .
the chaps doing that were absolutely covered in lead from head
to foot . . . we used it not in ounces or pounds, but in
hundredweights.'   LG

'I was there all those years and I never had no lead poisoning
but lots of people, you would see them gradually turning pale
there.'   BH

'The Morris 8 line was a deadly affair actually, because you were
working in all the lead dust – you talk about lead in petrol – you
was eating the damn stuff in those days. And one chappie on a
particular line, the frontal bone in his forehead had just rotted
away, and they reckoned it was caused through lead. Arising
from that we did demand from the management that we had
to have a blood test on everybody. I think about 93 per cent of

the men on the Morris 8 line were susceptible to lead poisoning of some form or the other.' NB

Building the Union

After a struggle throughout the thirties, trade unions were established to improve conditions at Pressed Steel.

Roger Sealey works at Pressed Steel and is working on a history of the early days of the union.

'There were attempts to organise or get people in the unions certainly as early as '27. This went on to various degrees right up until virtually 1933, when various propaganda weeks were organised by the local Trades Council looking at Morris's and Pressed Steel and trying to develop membership. Certainly we're aware that the Transport and General had membership within Pressed Steel by about 1932. Only a small number of people but there was a membership and a presence there. The National Union of Vehicle Builders had a shop committee based on Pressed Steel I think by 1930 and the Amalgamated Engineering Union had an agreement apparently with the company in some form by 1930. So, you know, there was that ephemeral organisation within the plant but it wasn't really particularly active.

'The struggle for control started virtually from the start in a certain way. There's a record of a strike in 1930 over the issue of smoking on the night shift. It's always been a recognised tradition in the engineering industry that on overtime and on a night shift you could smoke. All the other times you were not allowed to smoke but on these two occasions you could do it. The management apparently posted up a notice saying "No Smoking on Overtime or Nightshift" and the nightshift stopped work. It's not clear how many people were involved – it was totally disorganised, a spontaneous thing, so people did react. People in a sense attempted to control their environment.' RS

'Of course I still resented the fact really that there was no – there was nobody that you could take any complaint to, that maybe you've got to fight if you want any compensation for accidents, and you could lose your job for being ill. Well, I'd come from a town which was trade union minded and my father was a trade

unionist and probably his father before him, if they were out then, and I resented the fact that I couldn't be a trade unionist.'
HE

The 1934 Strike

Poor conditions together with frequent lay-offs and short-time working led to a walkout one day in 1934, which developed into a major strike with lasting consequences.

'It was an extraordinarily hot month, July of '34, a very very high temperature – a heat wave. What really caused the strike was that when men and women went to get their wages, they found that their wages was right down on that particular week. They asked their foreman why was the wages down, he said "Because you haven't done the bloody work" and they said 'Well, as far as we know we have." "Well, you haven't, it's proved by your sheets you haven't completed your programme. So therefore unless you work you don't get the money." Well, of course the money wasn't all that good as it was, and with a big drop like that, that got them going and they said "We're not going in there tonight, if it's like that and we don't get much for it." '   AE

'At this particular period I was trucking. They started to come out on strike, I think the press shop came out first, and then the shears come out and then the assembly come out and all the time the most exploited people of all, which were the labouring department, were still working. Well, I took the opportunity to go around, trying to tell them that we should join the rest of our chaps and fight for trade union recognition, so that our conditions could be better than they were. Anyway, after a day or two of this on a Friday morning I turns up for work and I was told that they had no work for me. I said, "What? No work for me," I said, "when they're out on strike and I'm prepared to come and work?" They said, "Yes, what you are working for is the trade union, we don't want your sort in here, agitating. Out." So I had to go out. But anyway, in the afternoon of the next day, all the trucking department come out. So I did sow a few seeds of good . . . I regard as good anyway.'
HE

STRIKE AT OXFORD WORKS :: TRAINING

THE GIRLS ARE GAME

STRIKE ARE YOU?

THIS FIGHT IS YOURS GET INTO IT

BUS STOPS AT CARFAX MODIFIED AFTER INQUIRY

STRIKE OF 180 AT PRESSED STEEL

Clash Over Claim of 150 Men to Wages and Conditions

CHALLENGE TO OWN

A S a protest against alleged low wages in the press shop at the Pressed Steel Britain's Works at Cowley came morning.

Strikers picketed the Gates and men and all the girls employed in the sympathy.

At a meeting at mid-day the management that they would hold premises.

MANAGEMENT

EXCHANGE WITH TY RECTOR

rting-place for Headington be Outside Market

ANK'S PROTEST

t Premises on Both Sides reened from Public

PAGEANT AT PINK

WORKS NOT TO RE-OPEN ON MONDAY

PRESSED STEEL

OFFICIAL STATEMENT TO THE "OXFORD MAIL"

Details of Strike Committee's Claim for New Scale of Wages

NO VICTIMISATION GUARANTEE WANTED

Enthusiastic Meeting of Workers Held in St. Giles

THE STRIKERS' DEMANDS

PRESSED STEEL WORKS RE-OPEN WITHOUT ANY UGLY SCENES

ONLY ABOUT 200 MEN & GIRLS RESUME DUTY

Jotted by Massed Strikers as They F... Main Gate

LOCAL NEWS IN BRIEF

Interesting Items From the District

WEATHER FORECAST

LOUDSPEAKER BY-LAWS AT ABINGDON

Proceedings Can be Taken if Three People Make Complaint

PETITION AGAINST HIGH RATES

THE MAN WITH A LOAD OF MISEF

Abe Lazarus

'The year of the strike, it was very hot that summer, and we were going to go for a honeymoon but owing to this strike we didn't get that honeymoon. We were going to Ilfracombe, or Ilfracombey they used to say. And so we didn't go, we just came straight up to where we live now.'   AF

Abe Lazarus

A person remembered with admiration by some was Abe Lazarus, a Communist Party industrial organiser, who arrived in Oxford just after the strike broke out and inspired determination to achieve union recognition. He addressed meetings outside Johnson's café near the works.

'He was such a brilliant speaker that he was able to convince them of the necessity of a union and they started building it. He had hundreds of forms on a chair – I was up there to have a look at it. Most of the time we were out of work, you know, we only did about two days a week all the time, and we'd go up there on our spare days just to see what was happening. Because there was fights and all that sort of thing. Anyway, they had all these forms and they issued 'em out and they got hundreds to join. That was the big start of the recruitment in Pressed Steel in 1934.'   AE

'Now I've been interested in political speakers, I've heard Ellen Wilkinson, Tom Mann, Harry Pollitt, Ramsay MacDonald, Aneurin Bevan, but this Abe Lazarus he was the finest orator I've ever heard.'   HE

'Some says he was really lovely to look at. I can't see it. You know, maybe jealousy of one man to another, I've heard others say he was great but I couldn't see it. It was his personality, that really won me. He was so kind and thoughtful for everybody. That was his whole life, helping people. He was like that all through his life.'   AE

After three weeks of bitter confrontation the strike at Pressed Steel was over. Management recognised the Transport and General Workers Union and conceded the right to have a union but the struggle continued throughout the thirties and wages remained unstable.

'The important fact about all this is that you had two situations in Oxford – you had the Pressed Steel which was becoming organised, there were people from up and down the country, and you had Morris's but they weren't organised until midway through the war. It was mostly local people working in Morris's, it was just an assembly plant. All the muck and grease and everything was all done in Pressed Steel. There were so many accidents in the press shop it created all these feelings against management, that they had a full-time Home Office official based in the Pressed Steel and a lot of people have forgotten that. It built from all those disputes. We tend to centre on one or two of the disputes but when the Standard line started there was a dispute a day, a stoppage a day, and all kinds of struggles came out of it.

'They never got nothing from the management. They never gave you nothing. It was a constant struggle, you know, to get jobs re-rated and better conditions. You just *had* to strike in those days. They didn't give you nothing. As they say up North they gave you nowt. It was a constant struggle. A strike a day had to take place in order to achieve anything in the factory. Nothing went on without a struggle.

'Each time there was a struggle, there was publicity in the press and if one cares to look back and analyse the sort of trade union development in Oxford, it more or less, apart from printing work and that kind of thing, all emanated from the Pressed Steel. I mean Woolworths became organised, they probably aren't now. Marks and Spencers – all those places were all basically organised by people right throughout the trade union movement in Pressed Steel.' NB

Throughout the thirties further stoppages took place to improve pay and conditions and the rights of the trade unions. In 1936 a dispute about non-union labour brought Transport and General Workers Union membership up to 2,000, which was about 90 per cent of the manual workers in Pressed Steel. Union leaders were victimised; in 1938, for example, TGWU convenor Tom Harris was sacked, resulting in a long strike for his reinstatement.

Work and Lay-Offs

At their best, wages in the car industry compared very favourably with other industries. But the work was occasional, with frequent lay-offs and consequent fluctuations in income.

'I found that I wasn't managing very well, because I had been used to good money, you see, really more money than what he was bringing home. So eventually I ended up with having 13 shillings a week housekeeping. Percy kept the rest and paid the bills. But out of that housekeeping money I had to put all the money in the gas (for we heated, cooked and washed all with gas), as well as any odd things I wanted like stockings. You know, we didn't have very much money then, for you to buy any big articles.

'We didn't have a radio. It was not until nearly Christmastime before we got the radio. And that was only that we had saved up. We could have done it on the never-never, as they called it, but Percy didn't believe in that. And I remember that he came home and he'd got enough for this Bush (He would have a Bush radio!) And we walked all the way home to Sandhills with that radio. It was quite a big thing. And he was as pleased as Punch when he came in with this radio and put it on.'   AF

'Well, they were the joys of that time. You see, if you were able to save up and buy something. Especially when it was something out of the ordinary.'   PF

Two generations of the Fray family have worked at Pressed Steel, Percy and his son, John.

'What was emphasised to me when I was a child was how insecure working at a place like Pressed Steel was. Many's the time my father was on short time. Even as a kid you realised that he had to work hard, his clothing, as mother has said, was always quite a mess. He was forever burning his clothes when he was on the spot welding and these are the sort of things you remembered so, but nevertheless Oxford was a one industry town, if you wanted to earn reasonable money then it was Cowley, either Morris Motors or Pressed Steel.'   JF

'I can't say about the good old days or happy times and all that nonsense, I don't agree with that, because you didn't have much money, especially married with a family, you didn't have much money to throw around. Shillings counted, pounds – talk about pounds, but shillings counted. If I was shut out Saturday morning – which I was, most Saturday mornings, during the summer – it was 6 shillings, I lost 6 shillings. When you come to think what that firm was making and the millions going around, and you think of the likes about forty or fifty of us they'd shut out Saturday morning just for the sake of saving 6 shillings! What would the total be – I don't know, about £15 something like that – saving the magnificent sum of £15 – that was the sort of thing I didn't like. I don't see why it was right, or why it should have been. You couldn't do a thing about it though, could you?'   CY

'For a start you'd be lucky to do three days a week. You'd be in there seven o'clock in the morning and they'd no panels. "Right, come back at ten o'clock." Sit outside or have a cup of tea over at Johnson's, come back in at ten o'clock. "No, come back in after lunch." You'd go back in after lunch. "Come back in at three o'clock." You'd come back in at three o'clock and they'd get the panels out. Then they'd come round at five o'clock, "Overtime tonight," and if you didn't do it they used to fire you!'   BH

Car production rose and fell in relation to seasonal demand from consumers. This meant that few workers could work continuously throughout the year.

'I think you had to talk in terms of £4 or £5 a week which was a reasonable wage. You could, at periods in the factory, earn a wage like that. Nobody had a full year's work at all. It was part of the system in those days. There was a long period of work and then you were shut out for so long.'   NB

This short-time working was administered with a card system whereby men were laid off with a card telling them when (or if) they were to report back for work. George Weekes remembered a rhyme the men used to sing when the cards came round.

'Here we suffer grief and sorrow
In today and out tomorrow
Here we suffer grief and pain
Here comes those bloody cards again.'   GW

Wage Books

Alec Robinson's wage book shows how his wages fluctuated with the seasonal trade in the car industry. In 1929 his wages were peaking at £5 week. The general level of wages fell as the economy went into recession. In June 1932 his average wage was only just £2. 10s. 0d., or half his 1929 earnings. Although there were better weeks, the general level is well down. Alec worked out his average weekly wage for 1932 was £2. 14s. 5d.

'The money in those days was 50, 55 shillings a week day work, that was what it was then, but you earned a little bit more than that piecework sometimes. But some weeks were just two or three days' work. When I earned £2 that was probably only one day's work or something like that. It varied – you never knew what you were going to get, because you were paid only what you earned and if there was no material up there or there was some holdup or anything, well, you didn't get anything.'

AR

Alec Robinson's wage book

George Mason –
above and left
(centre)

The Diary of George Mason (1933)★

George Mason was a skilled engineer who worked for seventeen years in a bleachworks in his native Lancashire. When he was made redundant he moved to Cowley in search of work. He started at Morris Motors in October 1932. He kept a diary which gives an insight into the uncertain conditions of the period. The diary shows that between February and July he worked only twenty-six full days. The sixty-two days that he signed on at the Labour Exchange he called 'Play Days'. His wages fluctuated from £3. 12s. 6d. for the week just before Easter to 8s. 5d. for 27 June, his only work that week.

George was, according to his diary, sent home early on twenty-one days out of the forty-seven he worked between 20 February and 14 July, though he never seems to have been started for less than four hours, and sometimes he had as many as seven hours' work. He never worked a Saturday in this period. George signed on at the Labour Exchange twenty-eight times during these twenty-one weeks at Cowley; signed off once; and when he was put off over Whitsun for the best part of a fortnight, he went back to Horwich and had to sign on there daily. His insurance benefit amounted to 1s. 6d. approximately per visit to the exchange.

People left the North-West of England in the years 1931–6 at an average rate of about 7,000 a year. This was not so fast as Wales (22,000) or the North-East (24,000); and not so fast as the North-West itself had lost people through migration in the period 1923–31 (19,000). It was a well-beaten path to London and the Home Counties, where in the early and mid-1930s an average of a little over 70,000 regional migrants landed each year.

The Diary of George Mason

Personal notes

ADDRESS: George Mason, c/o 14, Church Hill Road, Cowley, Oxford

13 October 1932

First day at Morris Motors Ltd, Cowley. As a result of a wire from Katie [George's sister]. A change at least from running a bleachworks for 17 years.

———————

★The diary was kindly made available by his daughter Hilary Wood. It was transcribed and annotated by Stan Shipley, from whose work these notes are drawn.

First three weeks a bit slow, owing to short time. Afterwards bucked up a bit, and decent going up to Xmas. First two or three days at Katie's digs, then moved next door but one lower down to Jefferey's.

23 Dec.	1932 (Friday) Works close down until 2 January 1933.
24 Dec.	. . . Kate and I went to Horwich to meet——and Thelma at Manchester, and missed 'em. Wrong tickets.
25 Dec.	Xmas day with Thelma.
26 Dec.	Teddy Jones fixing my teeth up.
28 Dec.	Teeth finished. Flying visit to Uncle Percy.
30 Dec.	(Friday) Stayed at Thelma's until today and she and I came to Oxford together.
31 Dec.	Went to 'Electric'. Indifferent show. Katie and G at Headington.

1933

1 Jan.	Spent New Year's Day in Cowley, looking houses over.
2 Jan.	(Monday) Started work on the new 28 horse power car.
6 Jan.	Don't remember what I drew today. Bonus beginning to fall.
12 Feb.	Walk round Iffley Lock with Eddie.
15 Feb.	(Wed) Erecting line out till Friday. Short of engines for 25's.
16 Feb.	Lucky enough to get in on rejects. Finished at 3 p.m. Took out a 25 h.p. engine, but hadn't one to put in its place.
17 Feb.	(Friday) Wages (including bonus) £1. 17. 10d. Bonus a bit better, 9s. 6d. Evening at billiards with Eddie.
18 Feb.	Playday. Signed on. Fancy there's 2 days benefit due to me. Pictures this evening with Eddie. Some snow. Turner wanted (Bromley, Kent) mechanic for automatic amusement machines.
19 Feb.	(Sunday) Wrote to Thelma and to 2 jobs and 3 houses. Tea with Katie.
20 Feb.	Out at 12 noon. To Witney after dinner to Messrs James Walker, Blanket Manufacturer. Saw J.W. in person, and . . . engineer. Mr Pease . . .

21 Feb.	Working all day. Out tomorrow. Assistant Engineer, Napsbury Mental Hospital, St. Albans. Write medical Superintendent by 28 February.
22 Feb.	Out. Signed on. Exchange puts me in for Foreman Millwright, Canning Town, London.
23 Feb.	Out at 3 p.m. Club for an hour. Billiards. Wrote Thelma.
24 Feb.	(Friday) Out till Monday. Wages £2. 10. 3d. Bonus up 11s. 6d. Snowing nearly all day.
25 Feb.	No letter from Thelma. Signed on. Saw Katie off to Birmingham. Raining: ground like soup. Spirits like the weather.
26 Feb.	(Sunday) Bad weather again. In all day. Wrote Thelma.
27 Feb.	Working all day. 2 letters from Thelma. Wrote back to her.
1 March	Out at 12 . . .
2 March	Signed on. No news re Canning Town.
3 March	(Friday) Signed on. Wages £3. 2. 0d. Bonus well up 28s.
4 March	Letter from Thelma. Saw Evans, and have to see Moss on Sunday. BE Box 5842. Daily Telegraph. Printers Engineer.
6 March	Letter from Thelma.
7 March	Finished at 4.
8 March	Out.
9 March	Out.
10 March	(Friday) Finished at 3. Wages for 11 hours 19s. 3d. Bonus 9s.
11 March	Out. Saw Evans. 4 or 5 weeks. Wrote Thelma.
13 March	(Monday) Out.
14 March	Working.
15 March	Working. Thelma's birthday.
16 March	Working.
17 March	Payday. 14 hours. 27s. Bonus 13s. Wrong. Out.
18 March	Out.
20 March	(Monday) Working. Greengate & Irwell Rubber Co. Ltd, Canning Town, E16.
21 March	Working till 4. (31 hours). Going in on rejects tomorrow.
22 March	Rejects. Changing diff[erential]s all day. 8 hours.
23 March	Finished at 4. 7 hours.

24 March	(Friday) Finished at 12. Pay day £3. 1. 9d. Bonus 29s for 31 hours. 4 hours.
25 March	Signed on. Pictures with Eddie. Walked by river yesterday and saw Oxford's first racing boat, 1829. Big as a whaler. Canning Town job gone.
26 March	2 walks out. Wrote Thelma.
3 April	Working all day.
4 April	(Tuesday) Finished at 12. Round Horspath Rd. Looking at Benfields & Loxley's houses. 34 hours in, all due for bonus.
5 April	Finished at 12. A. Stapleton & Sons Ltd, 218 Stamford Hill, (London) N.16. Engineer fitter . . .
6 April	Working all day. Lecture by Hackett of Accles & Pollock, tube makers, Birmingham.
7 April	(Friday) £3. 10. 0d. Bonus 32s. Out till Monday.
10 April	Working all day.
11 April	All day.
12 April	All day.
13 April	(Thursday) Pay day. £3. 12. 6d. Bonus 33s. 6d. Left Oxford at 5.45 p.m.
14 April	(Good Friday) Arrived at Thelma's 3.30 a.m. On the Pike after dinner. Johnny Hollands at night.
15 April	In Manchester.
16 April	Walk out with Thelma.
17 April	(Easter Mon.) Picture house afternoon. Palais de Danse, Bolton after tea.
18 April	T. working. Packing and mucking about. Left Horwich at 2 p.m. 4.30 p.m. Manchester London Road. Arrived Oxford about 9.45 p.m.
19 April	Started work, finished at noon till tomorrow. 4 hours.
20 April	(Thurs) Final lecture of season Oxford Engineering club, discussion on Automobile Engines of the future, by Mr Nixon, P.S. Co. Ltd. Interestingly technical . . .
21 April	Finished at 4. Out till Monday. Pay day £1. 13. 6d. Bonus 16s. 6d.
22 April	Changed handbag for carving set, etc. Letter from Thelma.
24 April	(Monday) Finished at 12. Letter from Thelma. Doesn't like carving set.
25 April	Finished at 3. 25 hours. Go in Thursday.

26 April   Signed on.
27 April   (Thursday) Finished at 12. Pay day. £2. 9. 9d. Bonus
             24s. 6d.
28 April   Signed on.
29 April   Excused. Went to Witney again and saw Pease. Not
             encouraging. Letter from Thelma and birthday card.
30 April   (Sunday) Wrote to Thelma. 33 to-day. Walk along
             river with Eddie's camera.

 1 May   General meeting Oxford Engineering Club. Signed
             on.
 2 May   Working all day. 12 hours pay.
 3 May   Out at 12. Letter Thelma. Sent snaps and photo and
             letter to her. Hope she likes them.
 4 May   (Thursday) Working all day. Pay day 21s. Bonus
             11s.
 5 May   Signed on. Play til Tuesday.
 6 May   Letter from T.
 7 May   Went to zoo. Wrote T.
 8 May   Signed on. Letter from T.
 9 May   Finished at 4.
10 May   All day in. Pictures with Eddie.
11 May   Signed on. Letter from T.
12 May   (Friday) Working all day. 30s. 9d. Bonus 12s. from
             19 hours. Dance with K and H's Carfax.
13 May   Signed on. Letter from T.
14 May   Out with Eddie and camera.
15 May   House on Passington Road, nearly off. P.S.C. for
             sale. No. 8(?) Mallam Payne & Dorn 22s. 6d. all in.
             Signed on.
16 May   Finished at 12. Visited P.S.C.
17 May   Finished at 3.
18 May   In all day, working. Finished till Tuesday. 30s. 9d.
             Bonus 12s. 6d.
19 May   (Friday) Went to Horwich. Arrived about 10 p.m.
             Met Mr Whitworth of Pinchin Johnson. Very inter-
             esting man (in train between Birmingham and
             Manchester).
20 May   In Horwich. Packed furniture for moving to Oxford.
             Carriage £6. 5s.
21 May   In Horwich.
22 May   (Monday) Left Horwich at 1 p.m. after seeing T. to
             work.

23 May	Started work and finished at 5 p.m. till next Monday. Bugger it. Interesting letters from Tamplin's, Brighton and from Isle of Wight.
24 May	Signed on. Went to Brighton for interview. Exes paid. May or may not. On to Portsmouth for I.o.W. Spent the night at Y.M.C.A.
25 May	Crossed to I.o.W. for Freshwater and Whippingham. Saw Saunders. Don't know what to think of the job. Maybe or not. Left Portsmouth at 5.40 p.m.
26 May	(Friday) Back in Cowley by 12.30 this morning. Travelled some miles this week. Stored furniture this afternoon at Martin's, Union St. Cowley Rd.
27 May	Signed off for Monday.
28 May	Wrote T. Knocked about.
29 May	Working all day. Gammy head, bugger it.
30 May	Working till 3 p.m. Finished till June 12, bugger it. Paid 31s. 6d.
31 May	Signed on. Letter from T.
1 June	Another letter from T. Wrote back.
2 June	(Friday) Signed on. Drew unemployment pay 14s. Caught 12.55 to Horwich. Arrived . . . 6.20 p.m.
3 June	Picnic round Burnt Edge with T.
4 June	In t . . . with T. Don't fill it up.
5 June	(Whit Mon) Picnic T. Meeting of the Waters, Angelzarke.
6 June	Jericho with T. Bought swimming costume. 2 fires in Bury. Signed on travelling card, excused Saturday and Monday.
7 June	Picnic with T. Anglezarke. Always with T.
8 June	Blackpool with T. Had a swim in the baths in the afternoon.
9 June	Got references off [to] A. J. Ingham and T. Green, and wrote for job in Tims. Rivington in evening. Bitten to buggery.
10 June	Southport with T. Signed on travelling cards every day, except last Saturday and Monday owing to Office closed.
11 June	Oxford bound again, arrived Cowley 10 p.m.
12 June	(Monday) Started work at 8 and finished at noon until tomorrow.
13 June	Working all day. Letter from T.
14 June	Working all day.

15 June	Working all day.
16 June	(Friday) Signed on.
17 June	Signed on. Letter from T. On Sam Bennett's pillion to Wheatley re Brickworks job. Dip in the river.
18 June	Wrote T.
19 June	(Monday) Working all day. Finished till tomorrow week.
20 June	Signed on. Wheatley again.
21 June	Signed on. Letter from T.
22 June	Nowt. Wheatley again. Job doubtful.
23 June	Pay day £2. 7. 6d. Bonus for 24 hours 22s. 6d. Benefit _____ 10. 2d.

$$£2. 17. 8$$

24 June	Mucking about. Letter from T.
25 June	Wrote T. Mucking about.
26 June	(Monday) Signed on.
27 June	Worked one day. Finished till further notice. Pay 8s. 5d.
28 June	Signed on.
29 June	Knocking about.
30 June	No pay day. Benefit only 12s. 6d. Signed on.

1 July	Letter from T. Frigging about.
2 July	Baths with Eddie. Wrote T.
3 July	(Monday) Weather bluddy ot. Signed on.
4 July	Mucking about. To Long Bridge's for a swim this afternoon.
5 July	Signed on.
6 July	Mucked about.
7 July	Signed on. Benefit (U.I.) 15s. 3d.
8 July	Letter from T.
9 July	Buggered about. Wrote T.
10 July	Letter from T. Signed on. Wrote T.
11 July	Frigged about.
12 July	Letter from T. Signed on.
13 July	Buggered about.
14 July	(Friday) Another week off starting. Maybe fortnight.
15 July	Off to Horwich. Train late in Birmingham, only just in time for 2.50 Birmingham to Manchester express. Wonder if I will be in time for her to meet me at 4.50. Aye she met me awreet.
16 July	Walk with T. before and after tea.

17 July	Blackpool with T. . . . baths. Signed on travelling card. Walk up north shore at . . ., came home, went to bed.
18 July	(Tuesday) Signing on travelling cards all the time.
19 July	Southport with T. Baths on my own, T. not so well. Sent travelling card to Oxford.
21 July	Benefit due (U.I.).
22 July	Horwich holidays finish.
24 July	(Monday) Still in Horwich.
25 July	Received 4s. 1d. in respect of benefit from Oxford.
28 July	Benefit due (U.I.).
31 July	Received 7s. 8d. in respect of benefit from Oxford.
3 August	Interview at T. E. Marchington & Co Ltd, Dyers and finishers, Droylsden, re job as mechanic. Mr Taylor (Engineers), Mr Dixon . . . (Mather & Platt).
7 August	(Monday) Full week's benefit (15s.) from Oxford.
10 August	Got Droylsden job. Letter this morning. To Droylsden after dinner, and got fixed up with Mr and Mrs Leech, 114 Moorside St., Droylsden. (Co-op Butcher's).
11 August	(Friday) Made a start this morning at above job. More hammer & chisel work today than in 3 or 4 years. Assured full time work 12 months or more.
12 August	Working till noon. In Horwich with T. at 4.15.
18 August	(Friday) Pay day £2. 1. 4d. (Short).
25 August	Pay day £2. 10s.
1 Sept.	Pay day £3. 0. 2d.
28 Oct.	Afternoon and evening in Manchester with T. Sent her home to Horwich on 10.15 p.m. She can sleep in her own bed this time.
29 Oct.	(Sunday) At Droylsden on my own. First entries since Sept. 1.
13 Nov.	Working till 10.
16 Nov.	Working till 10.
30 Nov.	Letter from T. Got a house 37 Webb St, Horwich.
1 Dec.	Wrote to K. re furniture.
2 Dec.	. . . Working till 4. T. here for dinner and tea (Droylsden). Horwich evening.

| 3 Dec. | Seen the house. Wrote K. & Hardimans about getting furniture here. |
| 4 Dec. | Surprise visit by Thelma. Droylsden Pictures evening. |

George Mason got married the following year and moved away in search of more stable employment.

George, who had scarcely left Horwich before 1932, worked successively in Cowley, Droylsden and Peterborough, before reaching Rochester in Kent in 1936, where he worked with few unemployment interruptions until he retired in 1965. He died 10 April 1979.

Morris Motors in the Thirties

The Moving Assembly Line

The introduction of the moving assembly line was a major change.

'I should think that changed about 1929 or '30 when they connected the two mounting shops and brought the running platform what you brought your chassis in, and that was the year they had a letter to stay home until further notice, all this big building extensions being done. Of course when we returned to work and we'd been sent for they got the moving lines in for the first time, the real Ford system going properly then.'   MH

The new technology of pressed steel enabled the introduction of the all-steel body at Morris's and the phasing out of the separate chassis. Steel car bodies could be produced faster and in larger numbers, and the old wooden coach building skills were steadily replaced by metalworking skills; workers had to learn to use the great presses and to cope with the unremitting pace of moving assembly lines. At first bodies and chassis continued to be assembled separately, but subsequent developments in steel pressing and mass assembly techniques saw an end to the separate chassis.

In the early thirties Morris Motors' market position was weakening. In the twenties Morris had thrived on the medium-sized Cowley and Oxford. In 1928 Morris introduced the first 8 h.p. Morris motor, but attempts to make it the cheapest possible car – below £100 – did not make it a success. In the early thirties, Morris produced many different models, many of which were flops, like the Isis or Empire Oxford, and Morris cars fell behind in the market. The depression encouraged a trend to smaller cars. Morris Motors only prospered when Leonard Lord reorganised the works and concentrated production on a new small car. With the introduction of the higher-quality Morris 8 after 1934 business picked up. In 1935 Morris Motors Group produced 96,512 cars, just under one-third of the total British car production of 311,544 in that year. By 1937 Morris were making just five models in ten styles, and by 1939 Morris was again the largest car manufacturer in Britain.

The Boss

The image of Morris Motors as the creation of one man was widely shared. The company's publicity film At Cowley *explains how Morris*

'spent a fortune installing what was then the latest in technological advance. Moving assembly lines were now the thing, part and parcel of the same old tune, the same old story: economy in production, increase in output, cars for the masses. But today it needed a millionaire's capital to build cars. That was all right. By keeping control of his factories, by putting everything he ever made back into the business, by thrift and an uncanny judgment, Sir William had become a millionaire. More than a millionaire. The man who above all else hated extravagance, publicity and ostentation, was incidentally to become one of the richest men in the world.'

For the workers at the factory the benevolence and power of William Morris were keenly felt.

'Lord Nuffield didn't make his millions by men sitting on their arse and he wasn't going to let them. But I don't know, I think everybody was happier in those days than what they are today. You didn't get a lot of money. If you had 5 shillings pocket money you could go out and get drunk with that but you can't today. Again, there was a lot of houses and estates being built up and men were going more or less hungry to buy their own house, I bought mine.' GW

Lord Nuffield gave away millions of pounds in benefactions both locally and nationally.

'He was benevolent, yes. Because he gave ten thousand pounds away and he'd get twenty thousand pounds' worth of

Lord Nuffield at the
annual Sports Day

propaganda out of it. He was headlines in the press, front page every time he gave it. I think he was a clever chap in that sense. He gave his money and got all the adverts he wanted. He gave his name to it – cleverer than what some of these people are today at advertising.'   NB

'It was one of those bad times when there was a shortage of work and the men were still off and he was in Australia. The men knew he was coming back, they knew what time he'd come back from the station. They didn't shout or anything they just lined the roads just before he got to his house. It was said that he didn't know the conditions prevailing at the works at the time, and within about three weeks those men were back at work.'   MG

Sports Days

Sport was an important activity for Morris workers, particularly at times when demand for orders was slack and they were on short-time working. Morris encouraged sports activities among the workers and there were departmental teams throughout the company. The annual Sports Day became a major public event in Oxford. A programme was printed in 1925 for the first Sports Day. It was a highly organised and very popular event ending with fireworks and the national anthem.

Monty Gibbs was a keen sportsman.

'Each department went in for a sports section, there would be football, cricket, the one mile relay race . . . and all sorts of sport. I think fifty per cent of Morris Motors were gone over to sports, that's why we got such a jolly good workforce at Morris Motors in those days. Billy Morris, he encouraged sport . . . he was proud of his team . . . proud of his workforce.

'Through the athletics and all that we got to know the whole firm, it wasn't only our department. You could have a department at the other end of the works, now providing they'd got a football team or a cricket team we all met together on the pitches. We ended up training there together, that's why it was such a good place to work in those days but there's nothing there now. It's all finished.'   MG

Sports Days were family days as well and the tradition carried on until the end of the sixties as Rocky Claridge remembers.

'When I was a child we always looked forward to Sports Days and entering the children's events. It was a great family occasion to go up on Sports Day and you'd probably spend the whole day there.'   RC

Monty Hillier was a well-known local sportsman and he recalls the band playing on sports days.

'The band was fabulous. It only got me into trouble one year – the meeting was open and I was a local man and they were cheering me on which is not done under athletic sport! But what I was going to tell you, and I think I'm correct in saying it – they used to pay the band, and one year they thought they'd save a bit of money – "We give them beer free." So they gave this beer free and expected them to play from about two o'clock till about seven in the evening. They'd drunk it all by three o'clock, the band, and they came for another lot! They reverted to paying them after that!'   MH

The Band

William Morris sponsored a brass band. Men who could play well were recruited to work in the factory. Harry Simpson was a cornet player in the band and worked in the paint shop.

'I was working at Vauxhall's and I was playing with the local band, and with the short time that was operated in the car industry at the time – everywhere for that matter – I was anxious to get a more regular job, possibly with a band. And Morris Motors were organising their band and I thought to myself "Well, I've got a trade. If I can get in at Morris's I probably could play with the band." And so I applied to Morris Motors through their employment agents, their personnel, and asked if there was any vacancies in the paint shop, which was horrible. And although I was to learn later that there were no vacancies at the time, the personnel officer had asked the bandmaster if he was interested in a cornet player from the Luton band, and of course he was offered it for nothing, as you might say, and so he said "yes". So that's how I got to Morris's.
    'Morris was very keen on the band. We used to play at the agents' conventions in Park Lane, London, Grosvenor House,

every year, and he always made a point of telling the agents that we were all amateurs and that we all did a job of work in the factory. So he was very keen on that. You felt nice when he said it that way. You hadn't really been forgotten amongst all the agents and he made a point of bringing it into focus.' HS

'It was a fabulous band . . . People used to get in early from work to hear the band playing in the canteen.' MH

'Mondays, Wednesdays and Fridays, during the lunch hour, we would leave the line at the same time as anybody else and we'd get to the canteen and we would have a cup of tea, possibly a sandwich. And by about twenty past twelve we'd make our way onto the stage and then that would be the lunchtime concerts. Playing so many times a week and all through the year, or all through the working part of the year, people generally accepted. Because there was only the radio and so they were accustomed to listening to things rather than seeing things, so it'd be well received on the whole.

'The band has meant almost a kind of spiritual food as one might say . . . I got fulfilment and I was able to earn my living every day, I didn't ask for any more than that . . . Just the normal comforts of life and two meals a day – with a little bit in the bank to go on holiday.' HS

The War

The original Morris Motors had expanded into the vast Nuffield Organis-ation producing Morris, Riley, Wolseley and MG cars as well as Morris Commercial Vehicles. In May 1939 the millionth Morris car was completed. Four months later the factory at Cowley was turned over to war production.

With the onset of war, many of the men were called up to fight. Their jobs were taken by women workers from all over the country.

Mass production techniques were turned to the manufacture of a vast range of war goods from small aircraft to tin hats, from tanks to torpedoes. As well as manufacturing, women workers repaired damaged aircraft and recycled aluminium from wrecked war planes.

'There was 150 women and we had to work hard on those machines churning out these shell cases, they worked hard, the sweat just ran off of them.' BH

'We did all kinds of things in 1939: converting cars, the Morris cars that were built, fetching them all in, spraying them the Army or RAF colours, repairing lorries and that kind of stuff, and then after six or seven months they started to build Tiger Moths . . . I did some of that, then I left and went into the Navy.'   LG

'It was quite a happy atmosphere really. You know, although the war was on there was a great companionship. Everybody helped one another . . .

'There was one girl – a Swiss girl, I remember – when it got very hot, she used to tie a string round the airgun that was used to blow the swarf off the torpedoes and put it down her dress to cool herself off.'   PB

Peggy Burgess began by making torpedoes.

'I was moved over to the flight shed – I should think that was about 1942 time – and then I went to aircraft, doing the petrol tanks. We had to cover those with cloth, which was stuck on, covered with the rubber and then sealed.

'The money was quite good really. Of course we didn't get as much as the men, but were able to save a little bit, you know, and then spend a bit of course. I used to buy a few clothes but of course you couldn't buy many because it was on coupons, but if you scrounged off your father or brother . . .'

At the end of the war, the women had to leave the factories and the men were reinstated. They were issued with cards, some of which were brought into our shop.★ Production quickly went back to making cars.

The Morris Minor

Car production had continued in a small way throughout the war. When the war ended, car production expanded immediately, but there was no new model until 1948, when the revolutionary Morris Minor was introduced. A team headed by Alec Issigonis designed the Morris Minor, which developed into the Minor 1000, and became one of the most popular cars

★See below 'How we did it'.

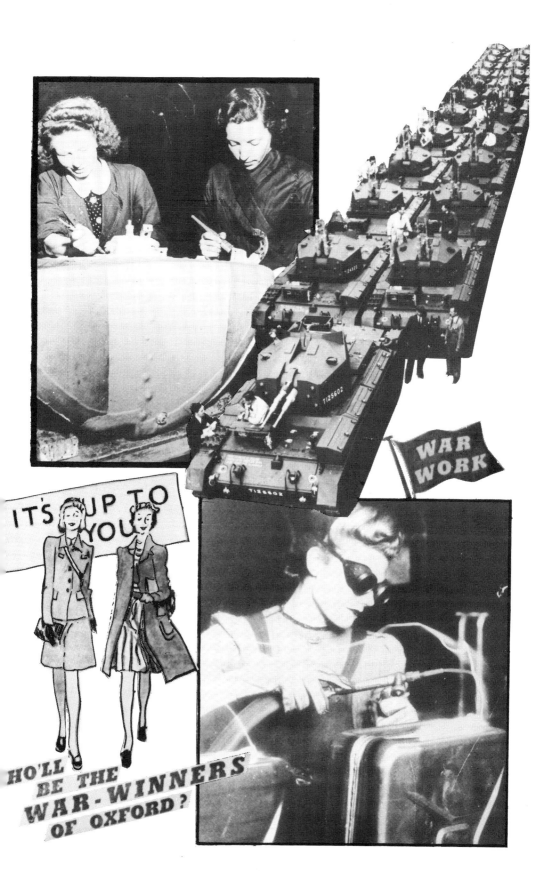

WAR WORK

IT'S UP TO YOU

HO'LL BE THE WAR-WINNERS OF OXFORD?

on the market, continuing in production for over twenty years, until 1971.
Designed to take advantage of mass production techniques, the Morris Minor
cost £280.

Reginald Job was the son of a village wheelwright in Claverdon, near
Warwick, and after training as a coach builder he moved to work at Pressed
Steel, where he learned to work with steel instead of wood. He moved
across to Morris Motors in 1939. Because of his experience in designing
complete body shells he joined the Morris Minor design team in 1944.

'I was given a one-twelfth scale model by Alec Issigonis. And
that was what I started with. And so I blew that up to full size
and laid that out on what we used to use at Morris's, a linen-
backed cartridge paper. Full size, you see. From that the
experimental shop made some jigs, they knocked up some panels
and that was the first car. It didn't have a proper rear seat, it
had a pan for two kids to sit on.

'You drew the whole outline and you drew everything. You
drew the templates all the way through it. Both in plan,
elevation, end view everything so that drawings can be made
from that half-size and sent over to the pattern maker who
makes the full-size model. And it's all, as I say, worked out by
surface development, which is a thing they don't do now.
That's why the Minor is such a beautiful shape – it really is, you
know. We tried to alter it once or twice, and it's impossible to
alter it because if you do anything to it you spoil it completely.
That's because one part bears a resemblance to the rest of it,
you see. It's not like the Princess today, I think as far as shape's
concerned I think its awful. That's my opinion.

'If ever I see anybody with a minor and they've stopped, very
often I fetch my Morris Minor book out of the car. I go up to
them, and I say "You fond of your Minor?" They say "Yes."
"It's a good car isn't it?" "Yes." I said "Have you ever met
the designer, one of the designers?" They said "No." "Well," I
said, "you've met one now." And I show them the book. And
they're tickled pink, you know.'   RJ

Working at Cowley

Bill Roche worked at Pressed Steel before the war and returned there
afterwards.

'I am one of those who was born a stone's throw from Pressed Steel. I was born and raised in Cowley – I'm a product of Cowley. It was natural for me as it was with other lads of my age to find myself working at the Pressed Steel, or perhaps one of the other factories . . . I went there in June 1937, which is forty-six years ago . . . I was fifteen.

'After the war you got a period when society was not booming, but certainly energetic, and there was this air of hope in society which to some extent was manifest on the shop floor. In the motor industry of course we had the whole field. There was very little imports. There was no motor industry in France or Germany of any degree, certainly not exporting, so that the home market which now has totally disappeared, or virtually disappeared, was all ours then. There was a demand for our products.' BR

'They were a good crowd of lads, nearly all of them ex-servicemen, and there was a good spirit of comradeship amongst them. They were all falling over one another to help each other, make sure that no work went up the line. It was a point of honour that you didn't let any work go by, that every job was done well, and that when the car got to the end of the line, it was a good car and we'd get a good name in the world for our cars.' LG

'I began work at Pressed Steel in 1950. I had come out of the forces, having been in the war . . . I went to work at Pressed Steel and I went from £5.70 a week up to £21 a week, so it was sheer economic necessity that drove me to the car industry. I loathed it.' DB

'I've always been a Cowley man . . . I came to Cowley with my father when he started in the car factory in the 1930s . . . Being thrown out of work after coming out of the forces in 1952, I made the usual pilgrimage to one of the car factories which turned out to be Pressed Steel . . . and I was taken on as a solder boy.' BJ

Although the men were given back their jobs, women continued to work at the factory.

'We were just in the minority – it was a job, the money was good in those days and we knew that if we grumbled we went unheard anyway at that time and so we just used to accept two-thirds of a man's rate.'   HJ

'We used to look like nothing on earth. We used to have these baggy boiler suits, what you'd see men wear . . . and we used to have to wear those steel-toecapped shoes . . . we all looked like Dracula's daughters.'   KM

'[the women] were never all over the factory, as they are now. They were during the war when there weren't any men, but when the men came back the women got put off again. That's always been the way of it . . . There were men's areas and women's areas . . . even sweeping the floor was a man's job. In the women's departments the women didn't sweep the floor, the men did it.'   JK

The British Car Industry 1930–1950

Cars produced per worker in the thirties

Morris kept almost the same workforce from 1924 to 1934: looking at the Cowley assembly plant in 1924 5,500 and in 1934 5,000, while car production rose from 33,000 to 58,000 and by 1935 had reached 96,000. Physical output per head averaged 6.00 in 1924 and had risen to 11.6 by 1934 while the average for the whole industry was 6.02. Morris employed about 8 per cent of all car workers and produced just under one-third of all private cars.

Car production in the thirties

	Morris	Total British
1930	58,436	169,669
1931	43,582	158,997
1932	50,337	171,244
1933	44,049	220,779
1934	96,512	311,544
1935	58,248	256,866

By the mid-thirties the profile of the British car industry had altered radically from the early twenties. The industry continue to contract: from 96 firms in 1922 to 40 manufacturers in 1930 and 33 by 1939.

The percentage shares of the big six firms altered as follows during the period from 1929 to 1939:

Morris	51.0	to 26.9
Austin	37.3	to 24.3
Ford	5.7	to 14.7
Standard	4.9	to 12.8
Rootes	-	to 10.9
Vauxhall	1.1	to 10.4

Post-war car industry

Morris Motors was the largest firm, accounting for 21 per cent of total production in 1947. Morris's estimated production was 60,000 out of industry total of 287,000. The industry employed 284,000 people in 1948. Austin Motors held 19 per cent of the market. Temporarily in 1948 due to shortfall in US production, the UK became the world's leading exporter of cars.

Austin Motors sales and profits, 1945-51

1945	£ 900,000
1946	1,000,000
1947	1,800,000
1948	1,100,000
1949	1,600,000
1950	5,200,000
1951	7,200,000

Morris Motors Profits 1930–1950

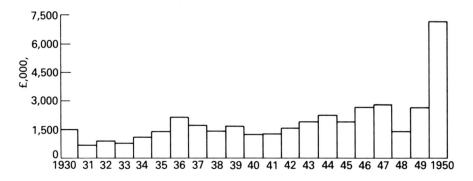

Morris Motors Sales 1930–1950

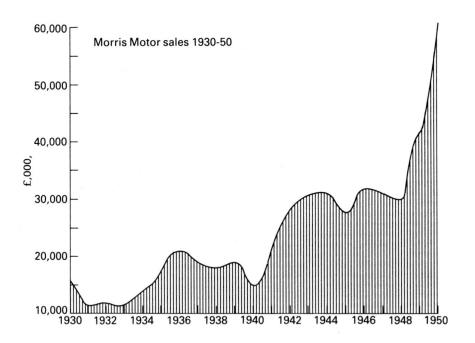

3   The Fifties and Sixties

Working at Morris Motors

In 1952 Morris Motors was merged with its rival, Austin Motors of Longbridge in Birmingham, and the new company was called the British Motor Corporation (BMC). The merger did not bring about a close integration of the two companies – the old loyalties of managers and workers as well as the customers to each firm remained strong.

In 1951, the average earnings at Morris were 4 shillings an hour. Profits in 1951 were £8.7 million. The workforce had expanded to 11,000 workers at Morris and 10,000 at Pressed Steel.

In 1952 the Morris Minor cost £375.

In 1951 Morris profits before tax amounted to £64,568,000.

The Unions at Morris's

Right from the beginning Morris had maintained a strong anti-union policy in the company. Despite the gains by the workers at Pressed Steel, across the road at Morris Motors workers continued to be subject to the anti-union paternalism of William Morris.

> 'In the thirties until the war broke out Lord Nuffield wouldn't tolerate a union at all . . . [There were] notices all over the place warning the workers that if they joined the union then he'd take action against them.' LG

Morris offered to send trade unions and left-wing organisers to Russia – all expenses paid – one way. Some organisers stood outside his factory with a megaphone every day.

Morris himself supported Oswald Mosley's New Party and the British Union of Fascists with donations.

'It was not really an industrial area as such. People weren't drawn

from an industrial section of the community, because this was
really a country area. Most of the workforce would be local, so
there was a general acceptance of enforced discipline. For
instance, you wouldn't be allowed to drink at your place of
work, or even eat, without some admonishment of some sort.
You could always easily get suspended for any kind of offence.
However, there wasn't too many "offences" about in those
days – people were glad to get a job. It wasn't like today, when
unemployment is suddenly a new experience – those people
had lived through a life of unemployment and they came to
respect it, or respect that discipline that could lose you your
job. You could even curry disfavour if your face didn't fit, never
mind about if you couldn't do your work. If you couldn't do
your work you'd be out. No question about that.

'These things didn't encourage people to take a stand about
trade unionism.

'In fact if your – if your political opinions were the wrong
shade and known to be the wrong shade, it would not have
stood you in good stead in short-time working.'   HS

'Whatever happened there if you did something wrong you were
fired on the spot – just told to get your stuff and get off the
plant, no notice. If you'd broken the rules it was off the plant,
and if somebody saw a man walking up the road between B
and C blocks carrying his toolbox it was a dead cert he'd either
been sacked or he was leaving.'   LG

'As far as Morris's was concerned there didn't seem many hopes
of organising Morris's, because the management always said
"If you join the union, then you revert to union conditions and
you'd be worse off than what you are now," which was
obviously a load of codswallop on Nuffield's part.'   NB

'Unions only seemed to make inroads into the factory during
the war years when – when everything or anything appeared to
be accepted to keep the workforce working. So certain licences
were allowed with regard to unionism during the war. But
after the war there wasn't an automatic acceptance of unions
within the – within the factory. There was quite a hostile
attitude towards unions in the beginning.'   HS

*The advent of war prevented further major strikes, and particularly at
Morris Motors workers gained increased rights under the Essential Work*

Order and representation through the Joint Production Committees. The unions had made some progress towards recognition, but Morris still opposed them and blocked their negotiating rights.

Morris was now seventy and in 1954 he retired to his estate at Nuffield.

The 1956 Strike

Despite the post-war boom, short-time working and lay-offs continued to aggravate relationships between workers and management.

In 1956 the companies responded to a government credit squeeze and a collapsing market for new and second-hand cars by making 6,000 workers at Cowley redundant. Pathé News covered the story.

'Saturation, the spectre which stands at the elbow of every boom, now haunts Britain's car industry. In the large Midland factories skilled workers who for years have been turning out as many cars as they can, find themselves working short time.

'On open spaces, on disused airfields, thousands of brand new vehicles are lined up with nowhere to go. Competition on the world market, and the credit squeeze at home, have hit the industry hard. Waiting lists for new cars are a thing of the past. And this in turn has hit the second-hand market. Dealers are offering every kind of inducement to customers . . . a pleasant sight for the prospective buyer but all the same the symptom of an alarming situation in a vital industry.' (Pathé News, *Too Many Cars*)

'We were told that the order books were full – we were taking on new labour and they were expecting the whole factory to go on overtime. Within a fortnight notices was printed and put up right throughout the departments to say every man with less than three years' service would be made redundant. Now that shook us rigid after being told what we had been told and we called a hurried shop stewards' meeting in the canteen that day and discussed it and they said "Well, we're not going to stand for that, we'll strike against it." '   AE

'If only they had consulted the union and said what was going on. Everyone used to go into the office, but there wasn't a word said to anyone, and it wasn't till the four o'clock on the Friday that they came and handed the cards all out to hundreds of men they'd got to come and work here in the first place. Just slap them out like that, you see.

'It was one of those funny things. When the word

1956...

"redundancy" came out they didn't know what it meant and so some of the people I knew went down the Labour Exchange to find out what this word meant – "redundancy". "Well," the bloke said, "you're not wanted, it's as plain as that." ' CY

'Workers in the car industry had bitter memories of the pre-war pattern of busy and slack seasons and management policy of hire and fire. The worst fears of the BMC workers were aroused when management yyannounced on 27 June 1956 that 6,000 workers would be discharged within forty-eight hours.

'Fifty thousand workers were involved in the dispute [that followed] at the various BMC factories . . . A Strike Committee was formed in each factory.' (From E. and F. Frow, *Engineering Struggles*, Working Class Movement Library, Manchester, 1982)

'We had a rough time at Morris Oxford during that 1956 BMC strike. Out of 7,000 only 1,000 had come out. We knew though that Pressed Steel . . . had blacked everything and we kept mass pickets on the place.

'It was the support of the workers not involved in the BMC that did as much to win the battle as the ones that were on the gates outside. It began to snowball to industries not concerned with us at all, but who saw the justification of our strike.

'After weeks of gathering crisis in Britain's car industry the great strike is on. But on the first day thousands are still walking past the pickets at the factories of the British Motor Corporation, the giant Austin and Morris combine whose sacking of 6,000 workers led to the strike. In spite of this half-and-half beginning, the unions claim that the key sectors are out and that a few days will bring BMC factories to a standstill. To convince the waverers, union leaders address open air meetings . . .

'The unions claiming reinstatement or compensation for the sacked 6,000 blame the Corporation for not talking it over beforehand. The employers defend their right to hire and fire and say any redundancy agreement must be made at national level. Meanwhile our foreign competitors rub their hands. Someone must start negotiating and soon.' (Pathé News, *BMC Strike*, 1956)

'It was a bit frightening going up what we used to call scab alley. They shouted "Scabs," "Blacklegs," "Come out and join us on strike," and that kind of thing. It was a bit frightening. It was for me, at any rate. But as I say, I was young and there was just room enough to get in as an individual. You didn't look forward to going home at dinner time either. It was quite terrifying.' RC

Tony Bradley remembers the end of the strike.

'At the end of the '56 dispute we all lined the road and we all held our trade unions cards up and we didn't say a word, as all the scabs and the blacklegs come out of that place we stood there. But not only did we hold our trade union cards up, we held our heads in shame, and as the bastards walked out we just held our heads down like that. And over that, ironically enough, came an uprising because they were so shocked. They were so shamed. If we'd have given these people abuse it would have had the opposite effect, but we didn't, we just held our heads in shame that those people had sold their own colleagues, their own friends with wives and families, down the river . . .'   TB

The strike was ultimately successful in gaining full union recognition from BMC management and in negotiating the first ever redundancy agreement.

'The BMC committee and the people who supported us, we got together and we said right, we're not going back defeated knowing that there was more in than there was out, we'd go back and fight like the devil to sew the company up as 100 per cent organised trade union and that was one of the things that came out of the BMC dispute. Within a year we completely organised the factories, got them all 100 per cent.

'The unions settled the strike with the first redundancy agreement in England. It gave us the basis for the future and from that time onwards we never had a redundancy again until 1966.'   LG

In the following years union leaders were again victimised; in 1959 senior shop steward Frank Horsman was sacked, provoking another long and bitter strike, he was not reinstated at Morris's but he was given a job across the road at Pressed Steel.

Pressed Steel and Morris Motors

Why should there be such a difference in union organisation between the two factories – Pressed Steel which makes the car bodies and Morris Motors which assembles and finishes the cars? In Pressed Steel the unions had won recognition in the 1934 strike. It was not until 1956 that the same recognition was won at Morris Motors.

'There is an extraordinary difference – certainly as an outsider, and I was only there for five years – between the two factories. The width of the bypass away, the same sort of people working in both and yet the most incredible difference in trade union activity.'   TR

'When Morris's started up it based its production very much on the old coach building methods. It started with wood building and at that time there was a decline in the carriage building industries at Swindon and elsewhere. They drew a lot of their labour from Swindon and they brought traditional coach building and carriage techniques with them. Also in the trim shops where they were dealing with leather this was very much from that coach building tradition, whereas Pressed Steel was a totally new technology imported from the States. Pressed Steel also brought in a labour force from outside Oxford which had no traditional craft basis because there were, in the main, no crafts that could be applied to it. So apart from some members of the Amalgamated Engineering Union and the pattern makers there was no traditional craft basis for union organisation, and that's basically why you've got the differences between the two factories on the grounds of technology alone. They started from two different bases.'   RS

The Car Industry – 1950s

The fifties

The 1951 merger between Morris Motors and Austin Motors arose out of the desire 'to effect the maximum standardisation, coupled with the most efficient manufacture and by the pooling of factory resources and consequent reductions in cost' *The Times*.

Leonard Lord, managing director of the new British Motor Corporation, saw the merger as a defensive one against the American companies. Commenting on the merger he said, 'We expect keen competition, but we have a few shillings in the bank and friends who will lend us money. We are feeling pretty comfortable.' But the use of the car industry as an economic regulater led to difficulties for the industry.

In 1956 HP restrictions were increased, down payment raised and the business allowance on cars was abolished. Car output fell by 40 percent.

In 1957 output was 860,000 units.
In 1958 output passed 1 million.
In 1959 output reached 1.4 million.
In 1960 output fell by 40 percent in the wake of another government credit squeeze.

In 1956 BMC laid off one worker in eight with no redundancy pay. *The Times* called BMC's action 'unjustified provocation'. The *Economist* reported that Sir Anthony Eden, the Prime Minister, nodded vigorously when Labour members criticised BMC action.

The Sixties Boom

At the beginning of the sixties Morris was part of BMC with Austin Motors while Pressed Steel had contracts to produce car bodies for several other car companies. It was a time of success with high profits. The revolutionary Mini had been launched in 1959 and became a very popular car.
The press was ecstatic.

'Some Baby!'
'Great Car Sensation!'
'The Little Giant!'
'It's a people's car that opens up a new era in family motoring.'
'These new cars are sensational.'
'BMC cars set up a new standard in cheap motoring. Performance and comfort retained.'

The sixties saw the start of a period of change for both Morris Motors and Pressed Steel that ran through the sixties and seventies. It was a period of mergers and reorganisations, including a major change in the method of pay for the workers. In the memories of many it was also a time of decline.
John Power started work at Morris Motors in 1959.

'All I can say is that in 1960 in the assembly plant I think production figures reached 7,100 vehicles a week, which is 350,000 cars a year. In the assembly plant today [1983] you find the bulk of the people are much the same labour force as they were in the 1960s who could produce 7,100 vehicles a week. Yet the whole of Leyland is only producing now what one factory produced in the 1960s and the position must be very clear – it was much the same people. Now I ask this question, that the same labour force was capable of that production in 1960, why aren't they capable in 1980?' JP

Bob Moore was a line manager at Morris Motors.

'We'd got the 1100, 1300 range. We'd got the old Oxford going very well. They sold themselves so we were inclined to sit back on our oars and say, "Oh, they're still going," until it was too late and then this brought on this final decline. We weren't doing what we used to do. We had two lines on the 1100 and the maximum output we ever reached in eight-hour shifts, two shifts a day, thirty-five and a half cars per hour off each assembly line. That's seventy vehicles off two lines and we'd got three other lines as well. And in those days, you can take my word for it, we had 94 per cent of those vehicles going direct to the customer and they were the best cars a customer could ever acquire.'   BM

Piecework

The method of payment for the workers was called piecework. This meant that people worked in gangs and were paid for the quantity of work they produced. They were paid by the piece and not by the day.

'On piecework it was cut-throat. You had to watch your back. You had to make sure, you know, that there wasn't anybody at your back. You had to watch your money. There was a lot of tension – and I enjoyed it! I thought it was great. Piecework women are a breed apart from the factory women. I don't think the women in there now could work piecework, because piecework was even harder than going on the tracks. It was killing.'   JK

'We were working so hard that when we stopped at nine o'clock all of our nerves would be on the jangle, and we would sit there and literally our arms and our legs would be shaking. And it would be very difficult indeed to hold a hot cup of coffee as you would spill the coffee on your fingers, because your arms and your hands were shaking so much. That's how it used to be.'   DB

'Naturally if you was a pieceworker earning far more money than outside people at that time, you were obviously going to go in for a better standard of living. That was the object of almost killing yourself to earn that sort of money. So you began to run down your health, because I know personally, the physical effort needed to keep going month after month really took its toll. I've never been a very big person but I remember going down to about seven stone in weight. I was eleven stone when I came out of the army and went to work in Pressed Steel and I went down to something like seven stone eight stone by working the piecework system. It really did take it out of you.'   BB

WIZARDRY ON WHEELS

THE

Revolutionary

"QUALITY FIRST"

MORRIS *Mini-Minor*

1959..

'You used to get very tense with each other because you would be working to your limit when you were on piecework. And the slightest thing would cause a row and you'd be at each other's throats, even for looking at somebody the wrong way. I used to stand there and I used to look at one of the girls on another line and she just turned around saying "And what the hell do you think you're looking at?" And I said "Your funny face." So she chased me! My mother jumped in between us and said "You leave my Jenette alone." I've spoken to that woman since and I've said "Do you remember that?" And she thinks it's hilarious now. It wasn't funny at the time – she'd have killed me if she'd got her hands on me. She had a knife in her hand. She would have done.

'Two women went for each other once, they lost their temper and one of them took a swing at another and knocked the foreman out. And there was boxing gloves in the place all the next day! "Do these fit you?" That wasn't humour that was shared between us, that was getting on each other's nerves. It was a safety valve in one way.'   JK

Shop Stewards and Piecework

Each section of the line worked as a gang and was paid by its results. Shop stewards played an important role in organising production, often chasing up materials for their gang so that earnings would not drop.
Bill Jupp was a shop steward at Pressed Steel in the sixties.

'The people working on lines would be a gang. You would then negotiate with that gang and the management the price for the body for going off the end as a complete job, and that would be the price for the piecework. Over the years I suppose we developed an uncanny sense of how much a job would be worth to us, and we were able then to build up our wages and we had a very strong element of control over the job. We were in charge of it, you know – the management had paid us for the piece, everything that went after it, providing that we turned the job out OK at the end of it, that was ours. If we made any time on the job we were able to go home early. We were able to make more money out of it by the way that we shed labour, or the way that we negotiated for more money on engineering changes, etc. That also was ours. So that part of the system was good, because it allowed people to be in control of the environment in which they worked.'   BJ

'I well remember once when I went into the management to argue bitterly about some very hot and oppressive conditions that we were in – bear in mind I was part of the gang and therefore my absence affected people's earnings – now when I got back onto the shop floor some of the men said "Well, what have you got for us David?" And I said "Well, I've been in there to try and fight for improved conditions." "Oh, don't worry about the bloody conditions, have you got more money for us for working in such bad conditions?" And I said "Look, I didn't go there for more money, I went for an improvement in the conditions." "Ah well, we'll cope with the conditions, just try and get us more money." That was the atmosphere that existed at that time. The system to some extent got to the men.'   DB

'You could pick a shop steward – you didn't have to ask anyone what kind of a shop steward was on a section, you just had a look at the wage rates and the conditions and you knew what kind of shop steward was on the section. Therefore the activities of the shop steward directly and visibly benefited the worker on the track or job. It was very easy for workers to see the direct benefit of trade unionism under those conditions. That's not to say that we should laud the piecework system. The piecework system was very cut-throat. But it has to be compared to what the alternative to piecework has been, and that is a massive handover of power to management. So therefore even though it was a cut-throat system, on balance, given the trade union organisation, it was very much to our advantage. Remember of course that piecework was brought in by the employer. And when there was no trade union organisation piecework was the best system, because the management could determine the prices. But once the trade union movement gained strength, then the piecework system worked to the advantage of the shop floor worker and the employer decided that it had to go.

'In the early part of the sixties there was a very hostile relationship indeed between management and unions. Shop stewards were constantly very close to victimisation. It was impossible to do anything really without risking victimisation. You couldn't hold a meeting on the plant, you couldn't speak

to people on the plant, you had to be very careful what you
said to anyone because if they repeated it to management you
could very quickly be victimised. Management were constantly
on the rampage, constantly looking to victimise shop stewards.
Obviously as the trade unions grew in strength, then that
tended to be minimised. Today of course we're returning to
almost precisely those conditions within BL – well, we are
returning to precisely those conditions within BL.'   AT

Managers and Piecework

*Some members of management saw piecework as a suitable system, but it
did lead to a lot of arguments about the rates for the job which were
negotiated every time there was any change.*
  Eric Lord was a Managing Director at Morris in the sixties.

'I believe that piecework was welcomed and that the men
preferred piecework to any other method of payment because
they saw the direct result of their efforts in their pay packet.
The harder they worked the more money they had in their pay
packet at the end of the week. And it was their effort which was
directly related to their pay packet, and this has always seemed
to me to be a very fair and equitable way of paying people, by
their efforts. And they certainly worked hard for it. One hears
all sorts of stories about the fabulously high rates of pay in the
motor industry in those days, and they were high, relatively –
but my goodness, they worked hard for them and they earned
it. From the company's point of view, of course, it was
welcomed because it meant that the higher the piecework
earnings the lower that our overheads were. So that it was I
think to mutual benefit.'   EL

Tom Richardson was an Industrial Relations Manager.

'When the bits were there and the production rate was going,
the line hummed, the blokes liked earning the money. The
troubles came when they were constantly being stopped for
reasons that were inexplicable to them or not told them and so
on. If you had a series of days where the lines were stopped for
no reason, no fault of the blokes, then they would start getting
irritated, and all the rest of it.'   TR

'One of the things I learned, as I'm sure many others did in the period we're talking about, in the fifties and sixties, was that as long as the cars were going off the end of the line – as the management used to say: out the bloody door – nobody bothered. Nobody took any interest in you. But the moment we stopped work all hell would be let loose and there'd be management by the dozen pouring down onto the shop floor. "What's happened? Why has the production line stopped? Why aren't you getting the cars off the end of the line?" And we quickly realised that the way to make management appreciate the fact that we were human beings and not part of their bloody machinery was to stop work.'   DB

Working Conditions

Although thousands of cars rolled off the production lines in the sixties, conditions for the workers remained surprisingly unchanged, as Tom Richardson recalls.

'It was just terrible, and my immediate predecessor, or the first person to do the industrial relations job at Morris, had stopped one of the worst things. (No one ever really believes it.) In the men's lavatories, the hourly paid people's lavatories, there was no lavatory paper. You know, you didn't dare go to the lavatory unless you'd got your *Daily Mirror* with you. After an enormous battle he got lavatory paper put in there, but such was the opposition to that, that whoever had to give the order to have the lavatory paper holders put into the WCs there, instructed the carpenters to put the holders on the outside of the door so that everyone going in had to estimate how much they would need before they'd started. I took on the industrial relations job and then it took another struggle of about six months behind the scenes to get the lavatory paper holders put on the inside of the door. We're not talking about the Dark Ages, we're talking about the mid-1960s.'   TR

Management Weakness

Despite the apparent success of both Morris Motors and Pressed Steel there were underlying problems that were steadily weakening the finances of both companies and laying the grounds for a takeover.

'We had started going down the hill. We weren't bringing out new models quick enough, I believe. Going back to the old Morris Motors days when we used to make a very good profit of around £30 million annually, some years as much as 55 million. If we were below 30 million we all believed we had had a bad year. Some people say the governor didn't give enough back to his worker, that he gave too much away to hospitals and charities. May well be they're right, because I don't believe we ploughed sufficient of our profits back into modernising our plant, into increasing and bettering our design staff and introducing new models more quickly.'   BM

'I used call it management by whim really. It was an astounding piece of incompetence, because all the cars we made I liked, and I never bought other than a British Leyland or BMC car. The Maxi was and is a good car, but it was ruined by such [management] incompetence. Of course the headlines in all the papers were about how awful the workforce was at Cowley, fouling up the introduction of this smashing new model. It clearly wasn't the fault of the workforce and I found it a great strain for four years trying to cope with that incompetence. Four years earlier the introduction of the 1800 went very badly at first, although again I think that was, and is, a good car. The story was (with considerable backing as to its authenticity) that the chairman and managing director of BMC, Sir George Harriman, had motored down from Longbridge's office on a regular visit to Cowley and had seen several of these 1800s on the way in a colour, "old English white", which he hadn't liked. (I remember it well after all these years – "old English white".) He got to Cowley, walked into the paint shop and instructed the superintendent not to paint any more old English white and then went off to see the managing director without mentioning this. Several days later there was an angry yelp from the sales director saying where's all these bloody old English whites, they're the only ones that are selling. And he looked up his production schedule and sees that – I don't know – three or four an hour, whatever it was, should be produced. So he called in the paintshop superintendent, who then told him the story that Sir George had cancelled the old English whites. Well, I mean if that's the way to run a large organisation then I'm not wanted in it really. I can't cope with such ways. I mean, after all, if all the public wanted to buy was cars the colour of old cow pats then that's what they should be, really.' TR

British Leyland

British Leyland

1967 merger talks with Leyland and BMC were encouraged by the Industrial Reorganisation Corporation. Agreement on merger was reached in 1968 with the aid of a £25 million loan from IRC. BL sales in 1968 were $1.9 billion, Volkswagen's were $2.5 billion, Fiat's were $1.7 billion. In terms of model ranges and productivity BL was weak. It produced twice as many models as General Motors but produced only one-fifth as many cars.

UK vehicle production
1967   1.552m cars
1968   1.816m
1969   1.717m
1970   1.641m

Car Industry Profits 1950–1970

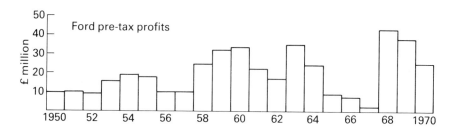

B.M.C. → British Leyland

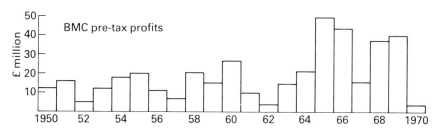

The Merger with Leyland

Morris Motors and Austin Motors had merged in 1952 to create the British Motor Corporation, and in 1965 Pressed Steel had been brought into the combine. Lack of investment, increased competition and poor labour relations meant that BMC was in a weak financial position. In 1968 the government encouraged and financially assisted the takeover of both Pressed Steel and Morris Motors by Leyland, a profitable bus and truck company chaired by Donald Stokes. The merger was also part of the government's policy to encourage the trend to larger concentrations of capital to meet foreign competition.

As a result of the merger with British Leyland, many changes were made to the organisation and management of the Cowley factories.

'A tremendous number of things happened. All the new brooms came in and everybody got swept up into different little piles. The organisational changes were enormous. And then the biggest change of all was that they introduced a large central organisation for the various functions which took away from the plants their own authority and vested it away from the plant, so that the people who were then running the plants – and I wasn't – must have had the greatest difficulty in coping with this very new and different situation. Because it was not one in which they had been brought up.'   EL

'Everybody was reviewing everybody else. The amount of production statistics that were published were horrendous, whereas in the days when I used to produce them for Joe Edwards all I had to do was to signify schedules that had not been met and whether it was through our fault. (Because obviously if the customer had cut back the requirement we couldn't have shipped them anyway.) I simply had to make sure that those schedules where we had failed were asterisked. I didn't have to give him any reasons, because he had his manufacturing directors at the meeting to ask them what went wrong and more particularly what they were going to do to put them right. But in the Leyland days we used to have to phone Coventry in the morning, give them all the statistics, all the reasons for loss, right down to the detail of what particular part of the line had broken down if there was a breakdown. They used to put them all together in a great list and send them all back to us. They were reviewed at managing director level in the morning and I used to have to go and see the managing director and go through detail by detail what went wrong. He had to do it because his boss was likely to ask him. So, you see, in those first two vital hours in the morning we didn't really do anything positive towards setting up for what was likely to go wrong in the future.

'And quality control! The amount of paper in quality control – I've never seen anything like it. We used to say if there was a strike at a paper mill it would stop us more quickly than a strip mill. I think it was true!'   GS

The Marina

For British Leyland (BL) the launch of the Marina was a battle it meant to win. BL wanted to challenge the extremely successful Ford Cortina with the Marina, but at the same time the company intended to introduce a new method of payment and organisation.

4 The Seventies

Measured Day Work

Mass production of cars had been built on piecework, a system of payment by results according to a negotiated rate for the job. The BL management now wanted to introduce a new system of payment based on a timed and measured assessment by the management of the work to be done over the eight-hour shift. This was called measured day work.

Hugh Eccles had come from Ford to reorganise the parts division.

'We had a corporate strategy, and it was a long-term strategy. One part of it was to get away from piecework and have measured day work because in the days of piecework the shop stewards had total control over production. The next thing we had to do was to get rid of all the bargaining units. There were all these different tribes that made up Leyland, and each tribe had more than one bargaining unit. When it came to trying to negotiate wages they were leapfrogging each other. I think at one stage Leyland had over 400 bargaining units. And it was a long-term strategy of management to have, as Ford have, a central joint negotiating committee on pay. This they have now got. These changes have taken quite a long time to get in and have been against considerable opposition.' HEC

'Measured day work was introduced because the assumption as I recall by Pat Lowry, who was then the Industrial Relations Director, was that measured day work would have the effect of reducing disputes because it would take away the areas of dispute. Firstly because you could argue about piecework prices and times and that was an area of dispute, and secondly, as the shop stewards' strength was built around the fact that they could argue about piecework prices and times, it would undermine the strength of the shop stewards and allow a much more easily manageable labour force and fewer disputes. Now in many respects there were many of us who thought that there was a

78

need to move away from the quite naked piecework system we had. Many of us would have preferred some kind of standard payment with a bonus element in producing it. But no, they were not prepared to consider any alternatives. They knew what was right for the company and they insisted it must be measured day work or nothing. And indeed they forced a five-week strike in the assembly plant for the introduction of measured daywork. They were actually able to boast to the men that "Why are you striking because we're offering you more money to do less work?" But they were the architects of destruction of BL, the people who had this obsession with setting up a single corporation at all costs, out of different companies, with different histories and backgrounds, and then trying to bring a pay structure into all of its plants that didn't suit it and actually cost more money in most of the plants it was put in. And that was the destruction of it.' JP

At Pressed Steel the merger with British Leyland meant the loss of its contracts with the Rootes group, which had accounted for around 50 per cent of its output.

'We went through a period of eighteen months with practically no work at all. And we were desperate, frankly, at Cowley for more work. The company told us for the third time running that they were going to introduce a new model into Cowley, the Marina, but it would not be produced on piecework. It would be produced on what they called measured day work. We fought this for all we were worth because we saw this as industrial blackmail. And we fought it bitterly for a long period of time. I mean fighting it by arguments across a table in negotiations. We eventually got to the point where the men were saying to us "Look, we've had eighteen months of serious short time." Some men were down to about £15 or £16 a week. This is in 1970. "We really must have this new model, and we're not prepared to call the management's bluff. We want that Marina in this plant. So you'd better do some negotiations and get the best deal you can." ' DB

Negotiating this deal took more than a year at both Morris Motors and Pressed Steel. Tony Williamson remembers one of the pay bargaining sessions in 1972.

'We started at half past ten in the morning with formal

negotiations which got precisely nowhere before lunch. They gave us quite a good lunch – in the hope, I suppose, that we would mellow a bit. In the afternoon we didn't really get anywhere very much. The management were in one quite large room which we went into to meet them when we were having joint meetings. We had a bedroom where the beds had all been tipped up on their ends and a table put in the middle, where we could retire and discuss things. At about five o'clock the bedroom was needed for other purposes, so we were then left sitting round in the bars or in the corridors or somewhere. In the evening the talks started to get serious and make some sort of progress, mainly with just Moss Evans (TGWU) and Pat Lowry (BL). I was not in the picture – we were sort of hanging around waiting, and then Moss Evans would come back and report to us a little bit and then go off again. Then finally just around midnight, Moss came back with a serious package for us to consider. We needed some peace and quiet to consider it. So we looked around for somewhere to go and the only place where we could meet to consider this was the bathroom. So we solemnly sat down to try and consider this, with one sitting on the toilet, one on the bath, one on the window sill – and Moss, I think, was sort of striding up and down the two feet at the end the bathroom.'   TW

After a five-week strike at Morris's and many months of bargaining, measured day work was introduced, but some of the managers at Morris's still had reservations about the new system.

'I can only speak for myself, and I was very apprehensive about the introduction of measured day work because I felt that introducing it into a plant which had been brought up and had been running on piecework for very many years was going to give so many problems, or that it would take years and years before it settled down. And I personally have never been an advocate of measured day work, because people do not see the results of their efforts directly in their wage packets.'   EL

Protest

The introduction of measured day work by the management of British Leyland was seen by some as part of a wider and longer struggle for control over pay and working conditions.

'The only thing that really stands out is the fact that both management and the shop stewards appreciated the situation – they both knew what their objectives were, and they both admitted to each other what they were doing. There was no question of it being a battle that was raging with people who were denying it – both sides openly admitted this was a struggle. Management were saying "We are going to win." Shop stewards said, "We are going to win."

'The report from the body and assembly division first of all refers to the staff situation. At Cowley assembly there was an overtime ban with AUEW and TASS, and ASTMS had removed an overtime ban. At Cowley body plant and at Swindon and Castle Bromwich AUEW and TASS re-applied sanctions following a further rejection of the company's offer. In the works at Castle Bromwich there were eighty-two of the day shift on the Mini laid off because of the effects of a Longbridge sewing machinists' dispute. There were 249 day shift press operators on strike in support of 192 night shift operators who are in dispute over a disciplinary action taken against two operators, and 170 other day shift operators in the press shop were affected. And as far as the service division was concerned we had normal working.

'In the chairman's statement for 1976, the Annual Report, he said, "In BL, though relatively few industrial disputes have been directly concerned with pay, so many strikes have occurred with no benefit either to the company or to the employees that one is forced to the conclusion that the underlying reason is the desire to make a protest."

'This protest was, in my view, a protest against the capitalism and the democracy of this country. And the people making the protest were those who had the levers of power to bring things to a halt and to undermine the economy. And they were very successful.

'We recognised that if we were going to retain the initiative we would have a chance of keeping control of the situation. So we therefore would set about planning how we were going to introduce a method improvement. We might have to deliberately put out a number of dummy method improvements to negotiate with the shop stewards in order to get one that we wanted. We had to attempt to keep them sufficiently occupied with their own ideas of how they were to deal with management plans and intentions so that they were swamped, and to that extent we were able to keep going somewhat better.

Also we had dual-sourced, we had more hauliers, we had ourselves set up. We were a smaller operation than the assembly plants and we were able to make these changes, particularly as we were bringing in new methods and procedures anyway.

'On one occasion we were contemplating having to change the role of a particular plant – it was in the KD [Knock Down]* operation – and I wrote to the plant manager asking him for information on certain aspects, and my questions were with a view to changing the plant, and using it for a different purpose. As I might have expected, that letter was intercepted and a photostat was in the hands of the shop stewards in no time at all and there was an immediate walk out. So I was obliged to write another letter pointing out that I'd changed my mind and we had no intention of going ahead in that direction. I sent that letter across and the people came back to work. There was no actual discussion between management and the unions over this and, actually, in sending this second letter I also rang the plant manager to say that when he got it he was to ignore it.

'The men came back to work and we got the information we needed. It wasn't a major problem, but it was just an indication that everything you were thinking of doing and planning to do was known to the shop stewards, who would immediately react in some usually predictable manner.'   HEC

Peter Jarvis was an inspector on the assembly lines at Morris Motors.

'People seem to take it for granted men strike at the slightest thing. They do not. They can't afford to, for a start. I have never known a man who hasn't stopped and considered when he's called out on strike, can I afford to do it, because he's got a wife, he's got children, he's got a car, he's got a mortgage. He's not going to walk out unless he's got to do it. He's either got so angry, so frustrated and bitter about the thing that he's thrown his tools down and walked off with his mates, and quite often with those you can stop it and resolve it or get a promise of resolving it before they actually get out of the gate. Once they've gone out of the gate then they are in a locked position.'   PJ

---

*Knock-down operation whereby cars are shipped in parts to be assembled abroad.

The Work

Despite the introduction of new machinery in recent years the changes in payment and organisation that resulted from measured day work did not alter the fact that making cars is hard physical work.

With each new car, the changes through improved hydraulics, more powered tools, more sophisticated machine tools and those changes brought by automation increased the pace of work on the assembly lines.

Bill Roche began working at Cowley in 1937, and for the line worker there have been significant changes in working methods since the factory was built.

'Building cars was on a much smaller scale than we have today. The time-cycle as we call it, the length of time that you actually were working on a particular job, could be as much as half an hour. Your work for that particular body would take you half an hour. If you compare that with some jobs today, where a man has got a cycle of a minute or a minute and a half, and that really is the major difference today. It is so much speeded up, like old Charlie Chaplin in *Modern Times*, that men haven't got time to think at all, because if he thinks it's gone by. Now that really is soul-destroying. It's boring in a way that perhaps it wasn't in the early days. You had a certain pride in what you were doing, there was a certain amount of skill in what you were doing because you were vehicle building as distinct from today, frankly, throwing them together, and because it's gone by you have to throw the next one together.' BR

Bill Smith began working at Cowley in 1975.

'They've got pride in their jobs but they're not allowed to take too much pride or time in their job because they want the next job through. If a bloke can follow a car up all through the stages and have a finished product as a team it would be ideal. They can't work like that – you just haven't got the room. It is a shame, because you'd have an end product, whereas a lot of blokes haven't got an end product, they've just got this thing going by them every five seconds and it's just another thing, every five seconds. And as long as they get their wage packet at the end of the week it doesn't matter.' BSM

However fast the line moves, and despite more automation, line workers still have to use their skill and ingenuity.

'We had difficulty on a windscreen. One of three things was wrong, either the aperture of the body itself was wrong, or the glass was undercut, or the rubber that went round the glass, that went round the aperture, was not standard size. No way could you get the corner of the rubber to fit. Now, of course you're not going to get the job through, so some bright spark comes in one day with a load of tiny little strips of garden cane, cuts them up into pieces, puts them under the glass, puts the rubber on, and it still falls in. So he creeps up, puts the piece of cane over the glass that's pushing the rubber out – that goes over the aperture, perfect, went through the sealer and it sealed solid, never leaked. Those cars are running round now. Some of the modern ones leak, those don't. It's the cane that's keeping the water out! It's a case of a man devising a means to get the job out the way, because under piecework it's his money at stake. It's his job, it's his livelihood.'   JM

'You've been on the job for years and obviously you're qualified for that job. I mean, you're looking for the quickest way and the best way to do it, to do a good job you know and do it quick. If the management had come round to the workers and said to the workers, well, if there's any way you can see that we can do this better, we could tell them.'   KM

'It was hard – it was hard on everything. It wasn't just hard on build line, it was hard in the paint shop. In the middle of the summer when you were sweating buckets, they'd come round with salt tablets and give you a free cup of orange juice. It was hard on the trim line, when you were humping windscreens, windscreens for MGBs, and they'd all be encased in metal and there's just you trying to lift it and slip it into a body. It was and it is hard work.'   JK

'Some of the equipment that we had went back before the First World War. Presses, for example, were throw-outs from the American Ford Company before the First World War and they were still thumping away and stamping stuff away in the seventies. But of course the problem was they were so old that anything you put on them eventually worked loose, so that for example if you look at any Marina Traveller you'll find that the rear air vents don't fit. They never have fitted. They tried all sorts of things to make them fit, but they never did fit, and

Travellers as far as I know came off the line, certainly long after I left, with those air vents still not fitting.' PJ

A Decline?

'British Motor Holdings got too big. Well when it became BL it was bigger still, and the coordination of the whole factories didn't seem to be coordinated at all. Although they were supposed to be under one management, we were little individual branches fighting for survival, but you were centrally controlled. You couldn't make the decisions as you could in the very early days, you were the man that was paid for doing that job and it was your decision, God help you if you make a mistake, but when it became Leyland everything had to go to London to be sanctioned.' BM

Eric Lord was a Managing Director at Morris assembly plant in the sixties.

'I think that there were a great number of things, and very great efforts were made, and the same with staff with job evaluations and job descriptions. But the problem became that people were spending so much time in trying to sort that out that they took their eye off the ball, which was making motor cars. This was one of our advantages, that we didn't need a job description – we knew what our job was, and that was producing motor cars. And we all worked to that end. Once you start trying to do evaluation and bring in systems and procedures (and books and books of procedures have been written), it takes away so much of the initiative of managers, because they tend all the time to dive for the manual to see what they ought to do under these circumstances. And life goes by very quickly then. The lines are running, and you're losing motor cars if you're not careful.'
    EL

'Towards the end of my time if you was an operator on a line you didn't know from one week to the next who your boss was. And God, you never saw the managing director. They don't know who the boss is, they never see them. Well, in my days your first job was to be walking down the lines to say "Good morning" to everybody so that they knew who you were. And the General Works Manager used to walk down the line every morning – so they knew who he was. It wasn't a secret society. The top brass weren't untouchables. But it got that way in many circles towards my end, and I don't think that the directors on many occasions made the right choice to take over some of the jobs. They might have been with Ford, they might have been with Chrysler, they may have served some time in the States, but we'd got people equal to them and better, in my opinion, humble as it may be.

'I can only speak with conviction what I think, and I've always spoken from my heart, but there's one thing I shall always regret – I do hope that it comes back, but I'm disgusted and hurt to see the name of Morris disappearing. I think it's a shame – the old governor must be turning over in his grave, bless him – to see the name of Morris disappear and just see Austin/Rover on the flags at Cowley breaks my heart, and I'm sure many old employees would say the same thing. I was only an employee, I had to earn my living.'   BM

'I viewed the management with a degree of healthy contempt, because I worked for a company that in 1966 was producing over a million vehicles with 90,000 employees regularly turning in profits of 30 million or more, I think 32 million was made in 1966. Then we watched the team of assorted whiz kids come into the company and not only bankrupt it, so they had to go to the government in '68 and the government forked out £35 million pounds to make the merger, but then again they had to go for another £1,100 million in 1974 and I think the grand total now is approaching £4,000 million. So it seems to me – and I made this point to the Think Tank report on the industry – the thing is, we used to make cars faster, better and cheaper than we're making them now, and it struck me that that was the way we ought to get back to, those very simple things. Instead of that we had people with charts and designs and systems analysts and God knows what else, and in the end of it all, we seemed to be submerged by a great load of experts, you know, who knew nothing about anything really, least of all about making cars.'   JP

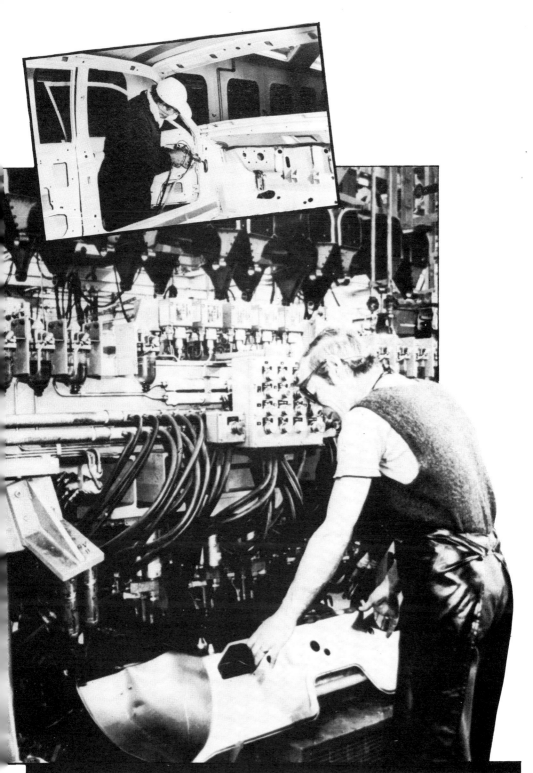

Bankrupt

There are two factories in Cowley – Pressed Steel and Morris Motors. Since 1968 they have been part of British Leyland. By 1974 British Leyland was bankrupt and the company was nationalised.

Many changes followed the nationalisation of British Leyland. It was a period of financial stringency and new styles of management.

. In 1975 the Princess was launched, but behind the glossy image the company was in difficulties. BL's share of the home market had fallen to only 24 per cent and the company made 1,400 workers redundant at Cowley alone.

The Image

Unprecedented media attention was focused on the company and its workforce.

Kathy and Johnny Moxham have worked at Pressed Steel several times since 1941 and do not accept the popular image of British Leyland and its workforce.

'But there's certain papers that I'm sure must have shares in the General Motors, Vauxhalls, Fords and everything else because they put the headline "British Leyland" and then "trouble" very big. But if the Japanese recall 450,000 cars, or Ford will be going on strike next week over the pay claim, we get two inches, not headlines.'   JM

'If something happened in British Leyland, no matter what it was, the next night or the next week some comic would hit BL and I used to sit and think well I'd love to have you and say, well, all right, you're there getting probably 800 to 1,000 quid for your half-hour. I'd like to get you by the scruff of your neck and take you in to BL, you know, and just say that's what we're stopping for. Would you do it?'   KM

'On the Line'

'You can't really imagine it, you've got to see it. You've got a man walking along a ramp about two and a half, three feet

Daily Mail

FRIDAY, DECEMBER 6, 1974   5p

SHIRLEY WILLIAMS AND LOVE

B.

Motor giant may need £50 m to beat cash crisis

LEYLANDS ASK FOR STATE AID

BRITISH L... ...ry's bi...
firm and ...
may ask th... ...
be help ...
The ...

STRICKEN EMPIRE OF A CAR GIANT

By PAUL CONNEW and ROBERT NE...

BRITISH
L...

Leyland

How the profits...

Ryder to study Leyland's future after £24 M loss B

By VICTOR KEEGAN, Industrial Editor

Sir Don Ryder, who is to run
the National Enterprise Board,
is to head a team looking into
the future prospects of British
Leyland after the group's an-
nouncement of a loss of almost
£24 millions last year.

This was announced last night
in the Commons by Mr Benn,
Secretary for Industry, during a
debate on a motion enabling
the Government to guarantee up
to £50 millions of bank borrow-
ings for the struggling British
motor group. This will see it
through until the spring, when
Sir Don's team is scheduled to
report. It is expected that the
Government will eventually
take at least half of BL's shares
...ange for injecting up-
... millions to en-

a loss because of strikes, notably
at the Rover-Triumph works. As
a result, the group is not paying
any further dividends beyond
the interim already paid of 0.5p
a share.

The corporation says that it
gave details of its five-year
investment plan to the Department of Industry and its prin-
cipal bankers in July. Although
the present cash position is
close to the forecast made in
July, the bankers had only
recently indicated that they
were not prepared to make the
necessary funds available. The
group has become more vulner-
able to inflation and strikes as
a result.

1974...

wide with a continuing track going over the top of his head, of cars, of which he has no control whatsoever, he can't stop them, he can't walk off. If he's going to do his job he's got to stand there – he's got say four functions to do with a very heavy windy tool, which is a thing two foot long, very heavy, on the end of a compressed air tube, with which he's doing tightening up. Now, he's doing that repeatedly hour after hour after hour, eight hours in the day, ten hours at night. He gets his breaks, short breaks. Now if there's not a foreman about, if the foreman's been called to a special meeting or the relief man's the other end of the track and he wants to go to the toilet, then in theory he cannot go. What's he going to do? He's not going to stand there and make a mess of himself, is he? Fortunately most of these little individual groups on the track had worked out a rota of their own, a couple of hours on and two hours off, this sort of thing. This is where you got this reputation of men going away hiding and sleeping.'   PJ

Night shifts were particularly difficult.

'I never came to terms with working nights . . . during the break I'd walk around the plant and I'd look at the sky. I can recall it now, looking at this lovely fresh air, and you'd think all the country's asleep except you, and I often used to say there must be a better way of making a living than this.'   HS

'One of the chaps I worked with for a couple of nights on that job, one of the things he said always stuck in my mind. He said, "If I ever thought about what I was going to do in this factory before I went in the gate at night, I'd never go through those gates." And those sort of sentiments made quite an impression on me. One of the most common was, what was it like working on night shift? People said, "The first twenty years are the worst."
    'On night shift you had your lunch break at one o'clock in the morning. I used to go to the canteen and try and eat lunch and go back to where I used to sit. (All the seats were made up by the men themselves – from bits of metal that had been bent into shape, welded together, bits of foam from the trim shop, bits of tape from the gum fitters and so on, to cover the rough edges.) So I was always sitting on top of oil drums, falling asleep. Then I'd wake up when the shift started again at 2, to do my job. But between 2 and 4.30, I'd be getting up, doing

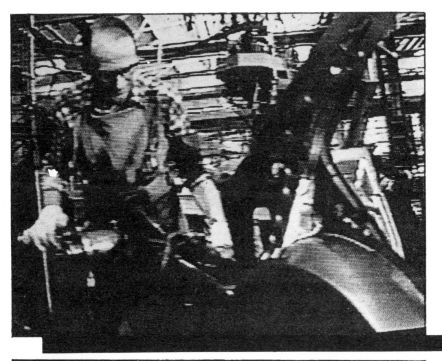

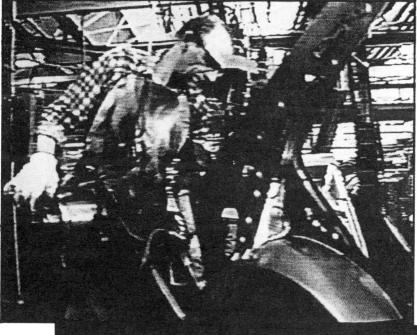

my spot welds, sitting down, falling asleep, getting up, every two minutes, and it was actually very draining – you feel very cold when you are having to wake up all the time like that. It was something that I never really got used to – some people do. It's in the nature of car factory production – they want to use the equipment as much as they can. So they will run a night shift where it's feasible.'   DL

'We were making the fascia panels and what we called the hockey sticks, which is outside trim, centre trim. It was the biggest money job for the women for a start, and we used to get some special orders in and the foreman used to stand over you while you were doing these, you know, make sure that they were A1 jobs. And you'd say "Well, what are these for, then?" And he'd say something like "Oh, they're for Daimler Sovereigns or whatever." "What are they for, then?" And he'd say "Oh, they're for some Arabs" or something like that – he always had the note with him who they were for. So we used to write rude words in the fascia panels and send them off. We'd often think "Well, there's some old sheikh riding about with 'Up the Palestinians' or something written on his fascia panel." We used to write all sorts of things depending on who they were for . . .
   'We did have one job on the MG, Prince Charles's MG came through and I think it took about 100 fascia panels before there was one that would sort of do for him, but you wouldn't dare write rude words on Charlie's! That's treason or something. You'd get hung for that.'   JK

The Ryder Report

In 1976 the Ryder Report analysed the continuing failure of British Leyland. Among many recommendations, the key ones were that further government investment in BL was linked to the performance of the company and to the introduction of worker participation in all BL factories.

'What happened in this country and had happened in BL, was that we had a load of people with plans and policies they imposed from the top down which were not relevant to the real problems that existed. What should have happened in Leyland – and Ryder made this point, by the way, in his report – is that ways and means should be found to harness the skills, the ideas, the energy, the enthusiasm of the Leyland workforce.

'Ryder also made the point that the ills of Leyland cannot be laid on the backs of a strike-prone or work-shy workforce. Now, that was the asset they had to build on, and instead of them going down to the shop floor and beginning discussions about how we can improve this, how do you think that job can be improved, how do you think this can be made more efficient – what did we have? We had the establishment of a Cars Council. People at the top sitting with directors. Then we had divisional participation councils, plant participation councils, all the feedback. And who sat on those things? The only people that sat on them were managers, senior shop stewards and shop stewards. No manual workers. No ordinary person was allowed an input into them at all. And none of that was done, and so we – we never ever tapped the skills, the ideas, the energy, the enthusiasm of the Leyland workforce.' JP

'I know in KD [Knock Down] I set the participation structure up, and I had very mixed feelings about it really. I remember at the first meeting we had we decided it would be a good idea if we all ate together, but the [union] reps didn't really want to be seen eating with us, I don't think (they'll probably slaughter me for saying that though), so we used to go off round to a hotel at Iffley and have lunch together. I believe that we probably got closer to them and they got closer to us as a result of it, but I don't think you can say "Well, we haven't had employee participation, and as from tomorrow we're gonna have it and expect it to go smoothly." It doesn't work like that. Life's not really like that.' GS

'The effect of Ryder on the shop stewards movement again was very dramatic because it was really an ideological issue. In a sense that the trade unions were formed as defensive organisations of the working class in order to defend and improve wages and conditions and to represent workers at the point of production or on the job. Ryder's scheme for worker participation was designed to switch that function completely, by making the shop steward someone who considers the problems of the company, particularly its viability and its efficiency. So Ryder set up a participation structure which was concerned with improving the efficiency and thereby the viability of BL. And so the shop steward comes to have a totally different role. When it was in confrontation, the labour force found itself confronting not actually the management but the participation structure and the trade union side of the participation structure. Which meant, for example, that on a number of occasions when there were strikes in that period the instruction "back to work" actually came from the trade union side.' AT

Women at Work

Not all car workers are men. Women have been making cars right from the beginnings of Morris Motors. Often they worked in sub assembly and interior trim work, but they also did the heaviest of work during the war. In the 1950s they were voted off the production line by the men. Not until the Equal Opportunities Act of 1976 were women again allowed to work in all areas of the factory. This gave the women workers legal support to break down the demarcation lines between men's work and women's work.

'Whether they stayed in the job was up to them but at least they had the choice . . . But before [the Act] they were just going to be out with no say in it.' JK

'In the forties and fifties, women didn't have much place in the trade unions, and I can remember that on the production lines, if there was an incident or an issue and they were taking a vote and women joined the crowd, we were often told "No vote for women." We used to have to go away – it didn't involve us even though we worked on the production line. But if it was something where half a dozen hands was going to sway how they wanted it, we were included. That's just how ridiculous it was. Looking back it's quite funny. It wouldn't happen today, I can assure you . . .' HJ

'I thought that it was hell on earth when I first went on there. One, because as much as I could shout about doing physical work I hadn't had to hump great big car bodies all over the place. There's a knack in pulling a Marina across the ceiling. Spot welding, we were in the training school to start with and we were taught how to spot weld and CO_2 weld and all the rest of it. And that's fine because you're only doing it in little bits of metal, but then you try and do it in a car. You have to

be a contortionist for a start, to do some of the jobs that's in
there. Jobs that men have been doing. You'd go up to the guy
and you'd sort of say "Well, I'm your spare man." That's what
they called them when they put you on. "Right, well, you got
to do this." "Yes." So they show you once and then you're left
to get on with it.

'There'd be tears. Everybody used to take their turn up in the
cloakroom with Winnie. You used to go up there in tears and
she'd give you a cup of tea and a paracetamol (or it was Aspros
in them days, it was before paracetamols). And you used to
get a cup of tea. She was more a welfare lady than the welfare
lady. That was a toilet cleaner. You used to go to her with
everything, you know. People would go to her and they'd tell
her that they were pregnant before they told their husbands.
She was a real confidante, you know. But it used to get into
tears, yeah, because it was a release. Saves you punching
somebody. Because you used to get so wound up that you could
be violent, you know, if you were that way inclined anyway.
They used to shout and scream at each other.'   JK

Beverly Smith worked as a spot welder on the Marina line.

'Obviously the men were on their guard but after a while they
realised that you weren't sort of embarrassed or anything. If
you let them know that as long as – like they used to swear and
obviously do things like that – but as long as they weren't
directing it at you I used to just shut my ears and say to them,
you know, "I'm not expecting you to change because I'm here.
You carry on and do what you want." But they were all nice –
I mean, you get the odd few looked at you and thought "Oh,
you shouldn't be here" but I didn't take any notice of them. On
the whole I think most of them didn't seem to mind. They've
accepted women in the factory now.

'We had to build the front of the car. You were building the
front of the car that went into the chassis to go onto the line,
if you know what I mean. That wasn't hard, because you could
work at your speed, where on the line it's moving and you've
got to keep with that speed, but also you've got to keep up with
the other men that are working with you, you know, you've
not to hold them up otherwise it gets a bit agitated, you know,
they sort of have to say to you "Can you speed up a bit, you're
keeping us behind" or something.'   BS

'Snowy was one of these people, what we call a stirrer in work, and sometimes what he thought was funny wasn't very funny. He just liked to think he was funny, and he used to keep on and keep on every time. He put the glass in the car, so me and Madeline worked in between him and four glassmen. He used to start trying to be sarcastic and going on and on. Well, one day he was going on and he took me on a bad day, I'd had a lot of problems. I stuck him for about I think about six or eight jobs and he kept going on every job. I'd had enough. He was just screwing up the glass and he was carrying on his chatter. Now I had a gallon tin of glue which I had to work with. So I picks up the gallon tin of glue and I thought, right, this stops you here and now, so I popped that right over his head. It just flowed down his face. I said, "Now, if you can't shut up, you're glued up." '   KM

'I think some of them did have this macho image that they felt, oh, well, they're great big men and they go home and they say to their wives "Oh, God, it was terrible in there." I mean, what's it going to be like when their wives find out that an eight-stone woman's doing the same as them? And she's just not going to believe them. She's just going to think, well, you know, you come home here, you're not doing any washing up because you've had such a bad day at the factory and there's my next door neighbour's wife's doing the same. I think that had a lot to do with it. Plus the fact they didn't want us on the same money as them. And with the Equal Opportunities Act came the Equal Pay Act. We were near enough on equal pay up in plastics but there was still that little bit of a difference. The men – and I think it's the same with most men, most working-class men anyway – they like to feel that they're just that little bit above their wives or women. Well, my own husband's the same. He doesn't think it's right that women are on the tracks.'   JK

The Edwardes Era

Despite the injection of public funds, British Leyland's position continued to deteriorate. In 1977 a tough new managing director, Michael Edwardes, was appointed to reverse the company's long decline. His two main priorities were to introduce new models as fast as possible and to curb what he and others saw as the excessive powers of the unions, particularly the shop floor stewards. There were many bitter and bruising confrontations.

'When the workers in Leyland had a legitimate pay claim, which had gone through the procedure with the backing of their national officials and in a ballot vote they decided if they'd take strike action, this management led by that little fascist Edwardes said "If you go on strike we will sack all of you, all of you." And that was when unemployment levels were considerably lower than they are now, that's the climate of fear coming from the top.'   JP

'There are three distinct stages over the past few years which I worked at the car plant over most of those stages. There was the transition from piecework to this so-called measured day work, which primarily – and there can be no argument about this – was purely and solely to cut manpower, behind the scenes, essentially to cut manpower. Unfortunately, the bluff of the trade unions was called and the men accepted it, they went back to work. The third stage was Michael Edwardes. He came in to do a job – whether you admire him or hate him or dislike him intensely, it makes no difference, he did the job he was paid to do. The unions were on the whole in the upper echelons quite aware of what Edwardes came in to do. Where they fell down was that they did not explain to their shop stewards – they did not explain to their men what that job was and the men never understood what that was till it was too late. They'd accepted most of the time by proxy what the management wanted them to accept through bluff and pure threats – they'd accepted and now they've suffered for it. A lot of us have left. Some of us regret it, some of us don't. We've gone our own ways, but the point is you cannot judge the car factory today on the standards of yesterday – there's no way you can do it. Conditions are totally different, and you're quite right to say that the men are not frightened of what the management can do now, they're frightened of ending up on the street where they know damn well they're not going to get another job within the foreseeable future – they won't.'   PJ

'A really important thing to realise is that the last thirteen years of this company is this. In 1970 measured day work was put in, it bankrupted the company, they went to the Government in '74, and for the last nine years the piper calling the tune is

BACK FROM THE BRINK

BRINK

1977...

THE BATTLE TO SAVE BRITISH LEYLAND

Michael
Edwardes

ACCLAIM

the general public of this country who are paying to keep this country running. Now I make this point, if the management is not accountable to the people who work for Leyland who are members of the tax-paying public, how can they be accountable to those who ultimately employ them, which is the whole tax-paying public of this country? In the last nine years public money has run Leyland without any public accountability, and during my time there we went to MP after MP, Cabinet Minister after Cabinet Minister, telling them exactly what's been said. We got an ever-growing army of industrial relations men, an ever-growing army of engineers. We've got an ever-growing army of office bureaucrats – what are you going to do about it? Because all it means, you've got to keep taking more and more public money. I hope people get this clear – this is a company that is run and financed by the general public. It's not run by Michael Edwardes and Ray Horrocks.* It's run by the public and this management refuses to be accountable to those members of the public who work for it and pay for it. That's the history of the last nine years of Leyland.'   JP

David Buckle has been a full-time trade union official in Oxford since 1964.

'If I were asked to crystallise my criticism of Sir Michael Edwardes it would be that I believe that he set out right from the very start with the idea in his mind that to achieve the commercial objective that he wanted, authoritarian system of management was required. And therefore that was the very opposite to everything that I believe in, in terms of the management seeking to achieve success by consensus, by persuasion, by discussion. He may or may not have been right on that. You naturally wouldn't expect me to concede that he was right. From the very beginning there was a very hard-line management push everywhere. And the days of reasonable meetings and reasonable negotiations with many levels of management ceased. On top of all of that, he introduced a system of communication with work people that was clearly – indeed, I would say blatantly – designed to bypass the unions. I think he saw unions as an obstacle to any progress that he hoped to make – and he clearly wanted to make very rapid progress. And so we had, for the very first time, direct

*Managing Director, BL Cars Ltd

communication with work people on a whole range of subjects without very often giving us any advance warning whatsoever. On top of that, he made very clear indeed that if closures of plants was what was required to make people bend to his will, then plants would be closed.' DB

'I don't think a climate of fear is necessary at all. I'm sure it's possible to work well with shop stewards as a manager and take them into your full confidence. As an observer I would doubt that this is now being done, but I have to balance this by saying that you can certainly see short term much greater efficiency at the moment. My fear is what's gonna happen in five years' time, because I simply don't believe that the trade unions can be held under indefinitely. I feel that the pendulum in the sixties had swung right to the point where the shop steward was wielding power, and now it's swung the whole way back to the other side. What I want to see is the pendulum in the middle for once.' CK

Some felt that the impact of Michael Edwardes on the company has been disastrous.

'I mean, to be paid the sum of money that he's been paid, £51,000 a year, to cut production by two-thirds! It's a mark of Britain's industrial success that all the media can record this man as a success, when in fact under his leadership Leyland's production fell by two-thirds. And its share of the market fell from 33 per cent to about 18 per cent today. So he almost halved our share of the market. And he also managed to shut down things like MG and so on which are all national known symbols, rather like Heinz chucking away the label of Heinz on their beans tins, you know. MG, a world known international brand name, and he actually closed that down. So he's an absolute disaster.' JP

'There were top-level changes of management, and the people who have come in are extremely efficient and very hard people, and I think the assembly plants are now run by a tough lot of managers whom I respect, but sometimes I think people working for them who could have been brought along and talents that could have been developed have gone because they haven't been able to stomach the hard-line approach.' CK

'They don't know who's who now, you see. This is the thing,
whereas when I first started up there in '71, you knew who your
bosses were. But they change now like flipping over pages of a
book. One day it's so-and-so and next day it's so-and-so, you
know. The only people you know are your foremen. They're
the only people you know. You could see a person walking
around in a suit and you thing "Who the hell's he?" And the
next minute the foreman gets called in the office and he gets
told so-and-so wasn't working. "Well, who told you?" "Mr So-
and-so." You know. The foreman's even flabbergasted because
he's never even heard of him and yet he's the new boss. They
change so quickly now up there. You just don't – there's no
personal touch now, whereas there used to be. That's all gone.
All they think about now – quite rightly so, in a sense, I
presume – is the manufacturing of cars. Okay, that is their
business. I agree. But it's also very nice to have a slight personal
touch with the men on the shop floor. With the persons who
work in the office. But that's all gone – you haven't got that
now. It's just numbers, numbers, numbers. Here you are as a
number. As long as you clock in at eight o'clock in the
morning, if you're on staff, quarter past seven for shop floor,
and clock out at the relative time at night, then you're all right.'
   BK

'I left in 1978. And very simply I worked then for the managing
director who left in the January and I was sacked in the March.
I use the word "sacked" because I don't have to pretend that it
was early retirement, because I wasn't trying to seek another
job, you see. That's not saying that everybody that left was
sacked, but I think that if you're in your early fifties and you're
enjoying a good salary and perks you don't readily seek early
retirement or voluntary redundancy. Not unless you've got
rocks in your head.
   'But now, quite honestly, if I saw Ray Horrocks I'd shake his
hand because I'm really extremely happy doing what I'm doing
now and he did me a great service. I'd have probably have been
in the cask or my coffin by now if I'd have stayed. I've no
regrets at all, but at the same time I mean I was fortunate and
could do something else, and I don't think it's right that
managers should be shovelled out like dirty old rags. I see some
of my colleagues who have been out of work for a long time
and a bit depressed about it all, and I remember them as being
quite good managers.'   GS

British Economy 1970–1983

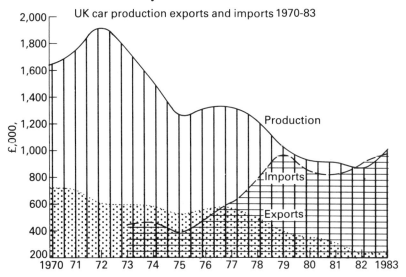

UK car production exports and imports 1970-83

The Car Industry

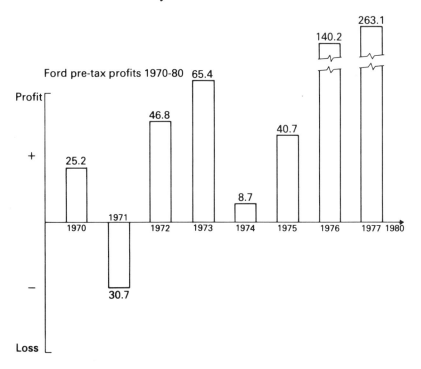

Ford pre-tax profits 1970-80

British Leyland

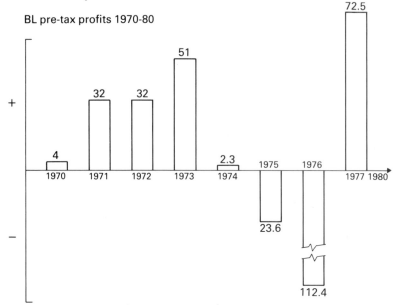

BL pre-tax profits 1970-80

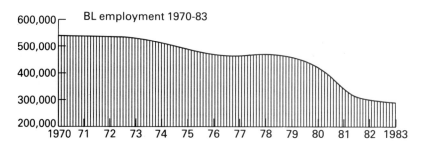

BL employment 1970-83

A deal with Honda of Japan brought new investment to Cowley. The Triumph Acclaim was launched in 1981. The introduction of new technology was a key element in the strategy of Michael Edwardes, as was his attitude to the trade unions.

The Unions under Edwardes

Bill Jupp was a shop steward at Pressed Steel for fifteen years.

'I think myself that the role of the trade union should be much more positive. I think that we lost our way through the sixties and the seventies, in terms of where we were going. I think we could have contributed a great deal more, if only we'd had the foresight and been prepared and had the guts to turn round and say, "Yes, we're going to participate in this and we're going to say that's the way it's going and that's the way it should go." Be dynamic and powerful about it because it was right. But we didn't. It was a negative approach all the time. React to what management had suggested. It should have been *our* suggestions, let management react to those – it never was, unfortunately. But, by God, if it had had been, I think myself we might have found something different, and certainly the trade union movement in British Leyland might have found a different path to tread.'   BJ

'My experience is that in most cases the shop floor are prepared to defend their conditions. And increasingly in recent years the leadership – certainly at national level, and also within BL at the highest level of the shop floor leadership – are not prepared to defend conditions or push for wages, because they get caught up with the ideology of the employer. An employer says that he's bankrupt, then they've no answer to that. They say "Well, we can read a balance sheet and we've got to be careful, we've got to compromise" and so on. Whereas a shop floor worker will say "I've got a balance of payments problem as well, how am I going to live? We just have to have wages and where is the money going anyway?" and so on.'   AT

'I always found that the national trade union officers were very much in favour of this national-level wage bargaining, national-level talk. I suppose it gave them a reason to exist, really. So they were always at one with the company in trying to draw away from the shop floor, and as they drew away from the shop floor, what happened was that the blokes had less and less interest in what went on. They couldn't influence what went on, and if you can't influence what goes on you take no interest in what goes on, and so on. So everything went wrong.'   JP

'Especially in the last year, people are definitely thinking of what is the point of belonging to a trade union. We're paying 50p a week so they can roll round in their Ford Granadas and have cosy lunches in expensive hotels. What do we get out of it?

We don't get support when it counts. We don't get any campaigning about anything. We don't get literature sent through. We don't get leaflets pointing out which way the company's going, or analysis from the trade union point of view. We don't get any of that whatsoever. I expect that a goodly proportion of people would happily tear up their union cards, especially when you get victimisations taking place.

'From time to time we did feel strongly about something. One famous occasion was the 1981 pay review, when it was personalised into us versus Edwardes and his umpteenth insulting offer on wage rates – 3.8% or something, absolutely minuscule compared with the rise in the cost of living. Then we had a strike, and the strike started I think around about two thousand pickets on the gates. It was the biggest number of pickets ever seen in the whole history of the factory. There was a tremendous feeling of solidarity right across the factory, right across Pressed Steel and both assembly plants. All the gates had fifty or a hundred people on them, tremendous! But of course for various reasons it collapsed.'   LC

'I don't think the people in there realise how much work they could get to do for how very little pay were there not a union. If they got rid of the unions up there – and I can't see it happening, but should it ever happen that either the 560 branch is got rid of or made weaker – then I think it would be disaster for the car workers up there. It would be – it would be a terrible thing. Because there's things like you get slip time to go to the loo. If there wasn't a union there you wouldn't get time to go to the loo. It just – you wouldn't get it. It was the unions that negotiated the tea breaks. It was the unions that negotiated the forty-hour week, or thirty-nine as it is now. It was the unions that negotiated an hour for lunch. And don't tell me that management wouldn't try and take it away, because they would. They're not a charity. And they wouldn't turn around and say "Oh, you have an hour for your lunch." No way.'   JK

Inside the Factories

Morris Motors and Pressed Steel are now part of British Leyland. New presses have been installed in the press shop, but the noise still makes an impact on new workers just as it did in the thirties.

'When you first go in the press shop it's a bit overawing because of the actual noise of the place, and the feeling of the place. If you can imagine about thirty express trains going by and the sort of noises – it sounds like that. You've got bins clanking along with steel wheels against concrete, full of loose scrap, all jumbling about. Then down the bay – I mean, that makes enough noise on its own. You've got three or four of those going round different lines. You've got the noise from the power presses themselves, plus the noise of the shears and the blankers and the cranes, it's just colossal. Then there is also the automation and the air, the jets of air that blow some of the stampings off the faces of the dies – it makes a hell of a racket. If you put it all together, you've got to wear ear protection or else you'd end up going deaf after a while.'   BSM

A lot of new technology and investment has gone into new cars produced at Cowley. Bill Roche has seen many changes over the years.

'As each succeeding model came through, albeit it took ten years in between models, nevertheless each one was different. Each time, there was an improvement in technology and new techniques and so on. But it was very slow. We are now beginning to catch up – certainly the new Acclaim today, for example, albeit it's Japanese and perhaps that is why. Nevertheless we have caught up considerably with the technology of others. Hopefully as the new models come through and certainly the Maestro that we're now starting on will hopefully make another leap forward. I say hopefully because that's in relation to being competitive. There is another side to it, of course, and that is manifest itself in so far as there are not so many jobs. You can't have both – you can't have the new technology and new methods of building and retain the same number of jobs at the same time.'   BR

Colin Kilpatrick was a plant manager at Cowley.

'It's noticeable in the way that the plants are running now, people are working flat out in those plants now. I mean, I now go into Cowley assembly plant in a completely different capacity, as a transport contractor, and whereas when I was a foreman I was concealing the fact that people didn't work, now people haven't got any time on their hands. You can see people working really hard, and I know foremen in Cowley assembly plant who are quite literally rushed off their feet. And if there was ever a popular image throughout the country that people working in the motor industry were lazy and over paid, they're certainly not that now. They're hard working and they're probably only paid an average or below average amount.' CK

The Labour Pool

Many people spoke about the conditions at the factories today, but one of the major changes from the early seventies is the introduction of complete flexibility for workers in the plant. Workers are now directed by management from section to section or into a labour pool as the pattern of work changes.

'There's now a constant attack, and all the protective agreements that were established in the sixties are now all gone. Workers are herded around now like cattle in those plants. The protective agreements, the seniority agreements, which were the most important protective agreements, are now completely gone. We're seeing conditions where workers that have worked in off-track jobs for thirty and forty years are given five minutes' notice to get onto a track. Often with medical conditions. Often working in a pit, with overhead conditions that make it absolutely impossible for them to do the job. And they're just directed totally ruthlessly after forty years with the company. "Get in that pit and do that job or find yourself another job outside." And I'm not exaggerating at all – that is what is happening every day. Every day in those plants. And the difference between that and what existed when the trade unions had power a few years ago is absolute difference of chalk to cheese.' AT

'Over the years you develop the knack of doing these jobs, and the physical effort is reduced – but, by God, when you go on there as a new person, it really takes it out of you. And the other thing is that you're not quite so adaptable now if you're put into the labour pool. I think that at one time or another we've all suffered this, the instability of the pool, of going onto various jobs. Some people are really shaken by that experience. I have talked to many people that have really been shaken. "God, I'll be glad when this pool business is finished. Don't know where you are. Don't know where you're going. Don't

Wash-up strike

Sta 2 8 MAR 1983

halts the Maestro

by John Williams

PRODUCTION of BL's new Maestro car was halted today when workers voted for an immediate strike — over "washing up" time.

The dispute at the Cowley assembly plant in Oxford threatens the success of the car that has soared as the key to

UK sales league after one of the most successful launches in car history.

The Cowley workers are being asked to give up their traditional three minutes "washing up" time at the end of their shifts, which they use to clean up and prepare to go home.

Talks had broken down and BL intended to put its decision into effect today. Instead it was confronted by

would lose 1000 cars a day, half of them Maestros.

Only a week ago the company reported that 1982 had been its best ever on the industrial relations front.

Mass meeting

BL is pinning its hopes of prosperity on the Maestro, as the company aims to break even th's year after running up massive losses over the last five years.

The car selling so well

ing off early. The company estimated that this could boost production by 14 per cent.

Today's vote, at a mass meeting, took the company by surprise. In recent months strike calls from shop stewards have been heavily defeated on the shopfloor.

Mr Bobby Fryer, the Transport and General Workers' Union's senior shop steward at the plant, said other issues were involved.

"Everybody in this plant is

BL strike jobs could go to unemployed

COUNTDOWN AT COWLEY

D. Mail 1 8 APR 1983

By PETER McHUGH and MICHAEL KEMP

A LAST-MINUTE union bid to end the Cowley 'washing up' dispute appeared to have hit trouble early today.

Engineers' president Terry Duffy hoped to persuade transport workers' leader Moss Evans to talk to Austin Rover chairman Harold Musgrove in an attempt to lift the threat of the sack facing the strikers.

But, after speaking to Mr Duffy, Mr Evans poured cold water on the plan, which included a proposal for BL to 'buy' the six minutes allowed each day for cleaning up. Mr Evans said he didn't believe it

day papers under the heading: Three Minute Warning.

Problem

The BL statement warned: We hope we don't have to look for other people to take your place. But it is a problem, we would face up to. We owe that to everyone else at Austin Rover.

Yesterday the company appeared to be ready to give strikers' jobs to redundant motor workers in an attempt to get the car lines moving again.

Certainly Mr Musgrove was in no mood for compromise.

Speaking in Coventry, he said: This strike is not about six minutes but about union officials

attempts to return to the time when our factories could only be run by trade unions and shop stewards' consent and that consent was too often unreasonably withheld.

"It is an attempt to turn the clock back to the days of the early 1970s, when their industry and dogmatic resistance to change brought them to anarchy and the British motor industry to its knees. When these spokesmen talk about the need for a return to sanctions that is not what they mean at all. They mean a return to them of the power of veto.

After Mr Musgrove's attack, David Buckle, local TGWU secretary said the strikers spokesmen said if begin to

weaker worker Harold Musgrove would be more successful as the manager of a factory in Poland because he is articulating the views of the Polish regime about their factories.

But Mr Duffy insisted that some solution could be found. He said his union was ready to try anything to head off confrontation with the company and added: There are not only 1,500 Cowley jobs at risk. We are talking about 100,000 jobs that could disappear.

By Thursday 1,206 workers are expected to defy the strike but by then recruiting plans from the pool of unemployed car workers could be swinging into action.

The three-week strike has so far cost the production of 10,000 cars with a turnover value of £70 million.

Recruiting

Austin Rover has been considering recruiting from the dole queue to get the production lines — and the new Maestros—rolling again.

A pool of 4,500 former Austin, Morris and MG workers who have been made redundant over the past four years exists near the plant.

They could be used to boost the ranks of workers willing to defy their union.

Austin Rover privately expects about 3,500—half the workers—to return to work whichever way tomorrow's vote goes. Over the weekend centralised managers received dozens of telephone calls from workers saying they would be back.

know what job you're going on." It could be a really hard one, it could be a reasonable one that you can adapt yourself quite easily, but I'm only here for a day and that sort of thing. "Where was you yesterday?" The whole conversation of a person in that position is "where were you yesterday?" or "I hope I don't get sent on there today" – all this sort of thing. And I think, God, is this life? You know, is – is this what we have come to?

'It shook me, the speed at which the line moved. And I believe it was something like thirty-four cars an hour, and you just had time to do the operation that you had to do, press a button and to see the whole chassis and floor disappear, into the next stage which was a robot that never seemed to tire. Believe you me, at the end of the day, at quarter past four – because that's running right up almost to that time – you were glad to see the end of the day. The monotony of putting eight to ten spots in two places hour after hour, minute after minute, was absolutely soul-destroying. And all I can say is, I sincerely hope that the future generations are not going to be faced with that sort of monotony in their lives. Because if that's so, God help them.'
BB

'You were put into the pool when you were de-manned. They had a pool on nights and there could be three or four hundred in there to start with and eventually it would fizzle out. You'd go into the pool, and every evening that you went in you dreaded going in because you didn't know which job you were going to be given, then after a while if they found you a permanent job, you know, it was great, you'd relax and think, "Oh, god, a job, and I know what I'm going to do." Towards the end even if it was a job you'd looked at and thought "Oh, I don't want to do it," you were just glad to be out of the pool and being sort of shoved around.'   BS

'I've always kept ahead of that pool, luckily. (It is luck rather than anything else.) I've known quite a few women who have gone on the tracks – not to hold any permanently, but when there was a pool, there was a large surplus of labour, both women and men in the pool, and some of the women had to go on the tracks and some had to do cleaning work. Some women had to go cleaning the toilets, and I was very scared that if I ended up in the pool I'd have to go cleaning toilets. I wouldn't have done it. I wouldn't, I'd have left. I was employed as a machinist, not a cleaner.'   TM

'Paywise, I think it's disgusting what they pay up there. I really do. At one particular time I believe there was a survey done, and I think we were on par with a fishmonger's mate. And that is the absolute truth – we were on par with a fishmonger's labourer! And that was a shop floor worker, and that was when I was working on the shop floor, I thought it was funny. I thought it was a joke, but they were very serious. It was illustrated in the papers, as well. It was a survey done. And we were on par with a fishmonger's labourer. I thought that'd be great and we're supposed to be the great British industry.' BK

5 The Eighties

A New Era?

In November 1982 Sir Michael Edwardes left British Leyland. In February 1983 the BL Maestro was launched with the slogan 'A miracle is born.' It was praised by critics and bought by customers. But changes in working practices and the legacy of Edwardes's confrontational management style produced the bitter four-week washing up strike at Cowley.

The Unions Today

'There's a lot of historians in Oxford would say that history doesn't repeat itself, it's always new. By crikey, we've seen it does! Because we were hearing about workers struggling to get their organisation recognised by management in the 1950s in the assembly plant. We were hearing about authoritarian management. We were hearing about management that had got their blue-eyed boys, and the people they didn't like. Well, here we are, thirty years on, and we have an authoritarian management and a struggle to get trade union officials and representatives recognised and given a worthwhile role. So here we are, at the end of a thirty-year cycle. The climate of fear in industry is there. Mass unemployment is there. The threat is that if you don't want your job then you can get out. If you're not satisfied with your pay you can get out. So in the car industry we've gone full circle in thirty years, and it makes me wonder what's going to happen in the next ten years in this industry, let alone the next thirty.' DB

While we were making the programmes shop steward Alan Thornett was dismissed by the company. The union claimed he was victimised. For trade unionists victimisation is an important part of their history.

112

'Alan Thornett is obviously somebody who is politically motivated, and a lot of people there are opposed to his ideas, so they're not really concerned that he's been dismissed, then the point is – the important point is one which most would agree with, he's a democratically elected shop steward and the company has managed to sack him. Now, if they can sack somebody in his position, the point is not lost on anybody – they can sack anybody, and this is part of this climate of fear that's built up over the last year or so, certainly a marked increase in that.'   LC

'We had, in those old days, just the same problem. Tom Harris was sacked at the Pressed Steel. It resulted in a strike, I remember that, but Tom didn't come back. The membership couldn't do it and we've had many – even in recent years, even in BL, big ones, and what did the membership do? They found themselves incapable of support because of the circumstances, so we ask the question that when they say and talk about the union, who is the union? When it comes to supporting shop stewards in difficulties of that nature, you do seek the support of your membership and that sometimes is lacking.'   BR

'You've heard of Arthur Exell, who helped to organise the Radiators. They were very strong and militant in their day. He in fact got the sack from the Radiators, and they couldn't find a position where they could support him. Not because they didn't want to support him, but because of the economic situation at the time.'   BJ

'Likewise Norman Brown, of course, he made a very valuable contribution. Norman lost his job and never did return to the car factory.'   PD

Norman Brown was a member of the Communist Party and worked at Pressed Steel and Morris Radiators from 1935 to 1947.

'I always remember Harry Pollitt, who was the general secretary of the CP. He used to say to youngsters like myself, anybody working in a factory, that when you're working in a factory you should be a good workman, and a good timekeeper. If you're all those things, and you don't do things that you shouldn't do, then when you get the sack the inevitable result is that you're sacked for what you believe in. And that's the way I've always interpreted what did happen to me.' NB

'Today I think people are frightened. Frightened of losing their jobs. Especially managers. Managers. (I'm not saying I'm going to keep mine after this, to be honest with you.) But by the same token, they are – they're frightened, I think. Because it's so tight. It's becoming very disciplined up there. I'm not saying it's not unjustified in certain cases. It is justified. You've got to have discipline working within a factory, because it's so vast. You must have rules and you must have regulations. But by the same token, rules are made to be broken. By God, *they* break enough of them, you know! And I think one of the reasons that they haven't come forward to help this history is because they've been looking over their shoulder thinking "Who's going to step in my place?" Let's be honest, there's enough people out there to do it. This is the problem.' BK

'The message I'm getting very loud and clear is this – that whenever the economic situation changes and the boot's on our feet, we are not going to forget what some management have done to us in the past three or four years. In the same way that the men earlier were talking about what happened in the past, and the way that it motivated them and moulded them for the way that they behaved in the fifties and sixties, then the men of thirty-five and forty – the men who are suffering in the car industry today, under the style of this government and Edwardes – the people are going to pass those stories down to their sons and their daughters, and they are going to remember these things in the eighties and the nineties, and the first decade after the year 2000. So what's being done today is bricks being put in the wall for all kinds of trouble in the future.' DB

Class Differences

'We're all sort of getting on a bit, perhaps. We think of the joy of the past – after all, we were young then – but I would hope that at some stage we'll talk about the future, and what we could do about the state of British industry, because this country is going down the pan. And manufacturing industry is going downhill very promptly. Two of the things that the car plant seems to me to illustrate very strongly, are probably the two worst aspects of our society. One is the class differentials within factories, and the second one is the poverty of the professionalism of British management. The class differentials are very clear in a fairly small place like Oxford, where you can have somebody who's worked on the line for forty years with no sick pay, no retirement pension, no holiday pay – or very much reduced holiday pay, longer working hours, earlier start to the day, different canteens and so on. I even found when I was in the management on the assembly plant that the men in the early workers' canteen were subsidising the management's booze for lunchtime. The booze was free for the management, it wasn't for the working blokes on the line and so on. That appalling class differential is very very clearly shown up in Oxford because of whole families actually working in a local factory, so someone can have been on a line for forty years, see their sixteen-year-old daughter go into the office, and on the very first day there she has more rights from the company than he'll ever have.'   TR

'In the particular factory I worked in, the workers had to start work at 7.15 and clock in. Most managers started 8.30 to 10 o'clock, if they started at all, that was – (and we know, by the way, because I used to spend some time every morning ringing them to see who was in). So we knew that about a third were out every day. And the managers, their car park was 600 yards nearer the place of work – they didn't have to clock in, they had a different car park and they had a works policeman to ensure that you didn't go into their car park. The canteens. We had a main hall canteen, and I would emphasise that the kind of work we were doing was not a filthy dirty job, that the office staff used the same canteen as ourselves. But then the management had to have three different canteens. They had to have a junior staff dining room, a senior staff dining room, and an executive dining room, with loads of drink cabinets and all that. Whereas we were eating cottage pie and chips and all this kind of stuff, they were getting stuck into all this good French stuff, steaks and goodness knows what else. We know, because our members cooked it. So it's not an allegation, it's a fact. The shop stewards used to complain bitterly about this, but as I said to the shop stewards, "Don't complain, don't be jealous about it," because as I said to the management, "The thing is this, doing sedentary jobs like you do, sitting behind desks, the last thing you need is high protein food. So it's going to kill you quicker," I said, "so you keep eating it." ' JP

'People talk about the difference not just between factories, but between skilled and unskilled labour. *There is no one in that factory who is unskilled.* They're hourly paid. It doesn't matter if he's a spot welder, it's still some skill. You'll find that the majority of skilled people, who served apprenticeships, will keep harping about the difference between skilled, semi- and unskilled workers. All manual workers are semi-skilled, they all have some skill, and that is a big difference. We used to argue about it when I went up to the machine shop, which is the apprentice area, and the office staff, the little clerks who had sat on their backsides for the last thirty years, would turn round and say, "These men up here deserve much more than the shop floor worker, they've served apprenticeships – any idiot can do a job down on the shop floor." I turned round to them and said, "Well, you're one idiot that can't! You can't even turn up for bloody work at quarter past seven in the morning!" They couldn't do the jobs, but I think that, given the training, everyone on the shop floor is capable of doing an apprenticeship, but there's that difference and it goes back so far. I don't know whether it's a craft thing or what the hell it is, but until working-class people sort themselves out, then God knows what will happen.' JK

'What we've got to ask ourselves is not about skilled or unskilled workers or what happened in the past, but what is gonna happen in the future. I think that we have too many classes. You got a class distinction of the unskilled and a class that's skilled. Then you've got another society which starts work at eight o'clock, not quarter past seven. It would be better if we got together as one class and didn't have so many differences and differentials as we have today. For instance, I was working for about twenty-five years in the Pressed Steel and my daughter had worked for about four days, and on the fifth day she weren't feeling well. When I come home from work I said, "Why aren't you in work?" "Well," she said, "I don't feel well." We were brought up that if you stood up when you got out of bed, you were fit to work. But the fact remains, that although I worked for twenty-five years, if I didn't go to work, I didn't get paid, but because my daughter was working in an office, she got paid. It's about time we abolished separate canteens for one class of worker and another separate canteen for another worker. We in this country must recognise that we're all equal, that maybe some have got dirtier jobs than others, and therefore perhaps they can't have a white table cloth in the canteen, but we got to abolish these inequalities. Until the whole society comes together and we all get the same privileges, then I'm afraid downhill we're going to go.'   HE

The Lessons of History

'You have what started off a small family firm – Morris. It then expanded within Oxford itself, spread to Pressed Steel. It then expanded beyond Oxford, and what happens is it expanded ridiculously under Lord Stokes, became swallowed up in a hole. The end result of all these outside effects is that Morris, the thing it began with, is the very name and the very thing which is disappearing in the end. Morris has gone, so that's what's happened, that's what's shown up in your history. The start up of a nice little family firm – whether you like the man or not – and the disappearance today of the family name and the factory itself which it actually produced.'   PJ

'Some of what is being said is true, but some of it is being exaggerated verbally – not totally, but when people say it's fear, the fear that is motivating people is not purely because of the management. It is because of the situation that the company is in. I'm not just protecting the company's point of view, although somebody's got to protect the company and the plants in Cowley because they're the life blood of Oxford. Everyone will admit that, but there's lots of people just knocking the place as if it didn't matter if it survived or not. There is unemployment of unprecedented levels now in this country, and that is the fear that is created in those factories. A little while ago if people were threatened with the sack it didn't mean anything, and people said, "Do what you like," knowing they could get work outside. It's only become so dreadful now because it's very difficult to get a job. All sorts of examples can be given of that situation. Although not everybody is frightened to death, because when I instructed a man to do something which was against an arrangement, he stood up and said that was not the agreement we had. Nothing happened to that man.

He wasn't sacked. I took the reply back to the management,
who did listen. This is not just a defence of the management
there, but to give an example that it's not totally Belsen or
some other concentration camp, even though it isn't a pleasure
like it used to be. There were good old days.'   NB

'I'm in the factory at the present time, and I think one thing that
wants to be brought up is the fact that the present management
really should be pulled over the coals for the manner in which
they are running the factory. Years ago they had piecework, a
man earned a good wage, the manning levels were set up by the
men, the men were reasonably contented in their job – but
now with the management and the way they're running, it's
nothing else but a bullying situation whereby we're being
forced out of fear to do jobs, and it's inefficient. Years ago they
made £33 million profit a year, up to £55 million profit a year.
Now they have to keep going to the government. You get less
production. You get more inefficiency. It takes five years to
get a job from the drawing board to the consumer where
beforehand it took three years. Nobody as yet has blamed the
management – I'm talking about the higher echelons, not middle
management. The higher echelons have never been blamed for
rank inefficiency. The middle management at the present time
are not being allowed to manage. Years ago you had an
argument or a dispute, and you went to see your shop manager.
It was negotiated in the afternoon, there was no strike, it was
settled and everybody back to work. Now any dispute at all,
it's got to go to Piccadilly House to get an answer. The middle
management aren't allowed to manage, and this is the
inefficiency.'   JM

'People talk about assorted whiz kids that came in. I think
"rapists" would have been a better term applied to them because
they came in, they up and went. They're like Arabs packing
their tents and away in the night. Unfortunately, it's the people
like myself who've been there for a long time and no doubt lots
of other people who've spent a lot of time in the company
who've suffered. Honestly, it makes me weep to see what has
happened there to what was a fantastic company.'   JH

'One or two people have mentioned unemployment as an excuse
for no action being taken. Well, I think that's a load of codswallop.
It won't stop workers going on strike. Go back to the thirties

when there were millions unemployed – look at the disputes and strikes that took place in Pressed Steel and in other places at that time. Unemployment is an excuse, I think, to try and bluff people into not trying to take any action. We're talking about history, and I think we could all learn something from it. It's no good just looking at history – we've got to learn lessons from history. The lesson I draw from the factories is that the trade union movement has weakened in the factories, and the sooner it gets itself together and starts organising itself the better for the working class in this city and in the motor industry in general.'   NB

'All this talk is beyond me, really. I've only ever had three jobs in my life. I was apprenticed to a plumber – I started that in 1912. I went into the '14–'18 war. I come out of there in January 1919 – I spent all my gratuity money so I went and got a job at Morris's. Well, all Morris's comprised of when I started was two three-storey buildings, and a tin shed about twenty by forty feet that was our despatch department. I watched the old tin shed extended and I watched all the rest built. But we was brought up to think the man as paid the piper called the tune, but that's gone today – I mean, the gaffers of today he's overruled.'   HK

'There's been all these recriminations about management, the unions and men, but I think there's one thing we must take great note of and that is that men worked faithfully in that factory for fifty years. You get this talk about loyalty to the company and the company's loyalty – it's eyewash to talk about it, there was no such thing, none at all. For years and years and years, we attempted to get a pension scheme. Now on one occasion we were told way way back when Edwardes was the manager up there, "Yes, you can have a pension scheme, but you won't get a wage rise for the next four years." That was the answer, and they said "You'll have to subsidise it yourself." This gives just some idea of what was going on. Eventually they said "You can have a pension scheme." But the only reason we got this pension scheme was because at that particular time the government were instituting the new pension regulations. Existing pension schemes were going to be topped up, but if the companies ran their own schemes they'd not pay so much to the state. It was cheaper for them to run their own schemes than it was to pay the normal contributions. I think the difference

is about £2 per week per man, and when you've got a large labour force like Leyland had at that time it was a considerable amount of money. Nevertheless – we got the scheme and men with fifty years' service went out that factory with 30 shillings a week pension. One man I'm thinking of in particular would walk to work from Tidlington when there were no buses, and that's what he got for his loyalty. Now, can you expect anybody to be loyal to a company for that sort of thing? I was on the Pensions Trustees Board, and I addressed the same remarks at the round table with Mr Horrocks [Managing Director] and all I got was a shrug of his two shoulders and a roll of his gold pencil. That was the answer that you'd get. The men up there now don't owe that company a penny. They've been exploited all their life up there. It was a fight from the day you went in. I went in there in 1949 and I fought and fought and fought all the way along the line. I was fighting for pennies on piecework, I was fighting for conditions. Men were dying of lead poisoning – nobody ever heard anything about it, didn't even get it listed as a dangerous disease, couldn't list it even as an industrial illness. Nobody would wear it. Men died of kidney failure – nothing was said about that. Can you expect loyalty after that sort of treatment? It was a fight for any man that went into that factory from 1949 right up until the present day. They know what it's all about – they don't owe that company anything, nothing at all, and any management that sits up there and expects loyalty from men after treatment like that must be dreaming. They'll never get it, and that's still going on now to this very day. I talk to men who are in that factory now and they couldn't care if that flag fell down. It's as simple as that.'
TK

BL'S PROBLEM PLANT

Why Cowley is idle again

By Arthur Smith, Midlands Correspondent

THE overwhelming vote by hundreds of workers gathered in the shadow of the sprawling Cowley car assembly complex to support an overtime ban by just 22 painters has brought to a head another industrial relations crisis within the Austin Rover cars group.

The robots installed in Q and P blocks as part of the multi-million pound investment to thrust the Oxford plant into the front line of international car assemblers now stand idle. Output of the successful Maestro and Montego models, regarded as the keys to the company's recovery programme, is at a halt. More than 2,000 workers have already been laid off.

The company believes it must clamp down on what it describes as "the Cowley assembly tradition of wildcat strikes." There have been 130 stoppages in the Oxford plant already this year—30 in the last three weeks and in a statement on Thursday the company complained that employees were "playing into the hands of a small minority whoe aim seems to be to 'disrupt production and breed discontent."

But Ivor Braggins, senior steward for the transport union, argues the decision of the mass meetings — as much a shock to the unions as to the company — "shows there

Flashback: the Cowley "washing-up" strike last year.

But most workers do not seem to agree. Vic, a fitter who has worked in the factory for [...] years [...]

lifted a couple of weeks ago when, after [...]

back to the unions to sort out given that the action is in breach of the unions' official recommendation. After secret talks between Mr Armstrong and national union leaders in London on Thursday, Oxford union officials are expected to take the initiative to secure a return to work. But it is difficult to see why the rank and file should suddenly heed advice already rejected.

Equally important for the company, each of the many disputes tends to knock back efforts to achieve a fundamental restructuring of shop floor representation, which both unions and management agree is important for long term peace in the assembly plant.

The problem is set out in dramatic terms by one leading union official: "Austin Rover has created a state of anarchy by attacking the trade unions at Cowley. They believed that a weak shop floor movement linked with strong individual discipline would give them control. Instead, they are confronted with a workforce not lacking in spirit, but which has no effective mechanism through which [...]

---

rs' militancy poses r[...]

[...]ent's la[...]lso the [...]nflation

[...]ne as a [...] manu-[...] two [...] proudly [...] supple-[...] lost in [...]ee had [...]ge of 6.7 [...]79 to 1.8

[...]ons had no [...]g for the [...] a two-year [...] year, not [...]ions negoti-[...]rivatisation [...]ased wage [...] in the

[...]e felt for [...]'s winter [...] to take [...]nts. Mr [...]onvener [...] plant,

have a model r[...] economies of s[...] Jaguar is expe[...] £100 million p[...] and, with over[...] its sales in the [...] the strength [...] against the poun[...]

The exact fir[...] of Ford UK re[...] of dispute betw[...] management, [...] tions are am[...] profitable of [...] operations.

Productivit[...] vastly increa[...] figures give[...] unions, the [...] has dropped [...] Ford betwe[...] by 48 per [...] per cent at [...] 77 per cent [...]

Ford [...] cent increa[...] at Halewoo[...] ductivity in [...] at 1.4 cars [...] it stands [...] old Musgr[...] Austin R[...] productiv[...]

BASIC WEEKLY PAY (£)	To Sept 1984	From Sept 1984*	From May 1985
Vauxhall	132.41	147.25	147.78
Skilled	116.22	125.19	131.04
Semi-skilled	102.96	111.51	113.29
Unskilled			

* Includes consolidation of £2 a week of existing bonuses. Bonus varies between £3 and £15 a week. Total rise worth between 8.2 per cent and 14.3 per cent, according to grade.

	To Nov 1984	From Nov 1984	From Nov 1985
Austin Rover	128.60	140.35	152.60
Skilled	116.60	127.70	149.30
Semi-skilled	98.90	109.15	119.90
Unskilled			

Includes £5.25 from existing bonus earnings in each year. Potential maximum bonus of £30 a week would remain. Average bonus has been £19.00 a week. Offer including consolidation worth 19 per cent over two years. Excluding consolidation, worth 15.2 per cent.

	To Nov 1984	From Nov 1984	From Nov 1985
Jaguar	128.60	141.85	156.00
Skilled	116.60	129.00	142.25
Semi-skilled	98.90	110.05	121.95
Unskilled			

Includes £3.75 consolidation of existing bonus in each year. Potential maximum bonus would rise to £42.50 in second year from present £30 a week. Average weekly bonus last year £25 a week. Offer including consolidation worth 22 per cent, excluding consolidation worth 14.8 per cent.

	To Nov 1984	From Nov 1984
Ford	142.98	148.32
Skilled	127.18	131.94
Semi-skilled	110.73	114.86
Unskilled		

An additional attendance allowance increases earnings between £7.42 and £9.59 a week, [...] grade. Offer likely to be improved at talks today.

6　How We Did It

At the Morris Motors and Pressed Steel car factories in Cowley, Oxford, people have been making cars for the last seventy years. In this book and the Channel Four programmes we have been making a history built from the words and experiences of some of the people who worked there.

The process of making cars has changed tremendously from its early days in Oxford. We wanted to examine the differences between the past and the present, but more importantly we wanted to record the experiences of the people whose working lives have been spent in these plants. We contacted British Leyland and the main unions, but we also opened a shop in the Cowley shopping centre.

The History Shop

We encouraged people to visit the shop, to bring their memories, their mementoes and their experiences to help make this history. Several hundred people called into the shop, some in response to appeals from local radio and newspapers. We interviewed people in various places around Cowley, either in groups or by themselves.

As the interviews were recorded we showed them to people as they dropped into the shop. And we played them to small groups. Drafts of the programmes were shown to participants before they were broadcast, and as much as possible we incorporated the changes requested and the additional information that was given. Finally we invited people to phone in at the end of the programmes and help make this history.

It was clear from the start that there was no single shared view of this history, just as there's no such thing as a typical car worker.

There are many kinds of people who make cars, so there are many different histories, and the car factory itself can be looked at in different ways. All of these views are valid, but all are different.

We opened a shop
in the Cowley
shopping centre.

We interviewed people
either in groups or by
themselves.

The problem for us was to capture and convey the varied experiences of the car makers at Cowley.

Towards the end of the series we held a televised discussion with about thirty of the participants in the programmes. The section entitled Lessons of History is taken from this three-hour discussion. We tried to encourage as many people as possible to come forward to take part in the project throughout its nine-month duration. Ellen Bateman (p. 6) contacted us after our appeal on Radio Oxford for workers from the early days. At eighty-one she just hopped on a bus to visit the shop!

The local newspaper the *Oxford Star*, through the enthusiasm of its editor, David Ellwood, became an important part of the project. For six weeks they ran photo-features and encouraged people to contact the shop. Harry Kerry (p. 8) contacted us after reading an article in the *Oxford Star*.

People brought photographs and mementos into the shop, which were interesting in themselves but which uncovered more information. Mrs E. Slade brought in the photo of the sawmill works. Her father-in-law is in the picture, which shows Morris's sawmill in the 1920s, where parts for the wooden car bodies were produced. Another visitor to the shop, Mr Fred Thornton, saw the photo on display and told us that he had suffered congestion of the lungs from exposure to sawdust there. He was lucky to be given a cleaner job by a sports loving manager, who wanted him for the cricket team!

Mr W. Williams brought in the spoof door banger stopper from the 'Modification Liaison Department', one of several notices knocking officialdom which circulated the plant. Mr Alec Robinson brought in his wage book records of the early 1930s, which show how the production line worker's wage fluctuated, before the union gained the guaranteed working week. Mr Stan Shipley sent George Mason's diary to us which he had transcribed.

Mr Len Hatton brought in his demob card which gave him back his pre-war job at Pressed Steel. Thousands of women workers who had kept the factories going during the war were sacked when the men returned to their peacetime occupations. Mr George Weekes brought in the programme from the first Morris Motors sports meeting in 1925. Several other athletes saw this in the shop and we learned a lot about the sports activities at Morris's. And a photo of the band brought in by Harry Simpson led to many fond memories.

British Leyland has absorbed a tremendous volume of photographs from Morris Motors showing all aspects of production. They are now held by BL Heritage, from whom most of the pictures in this book have come.

We talked to over 300 car makers in the shop. We interviewed about one-third again in their homes. We recorded over eighty hours of interviews and factory material. We have donated all the material we collected to the Oxford County Library, Westgate. The transcripts of the sixty interviews and video cassette copies have been donated to Ruskin College, and to Oxford Polytechnic, and to the National Museum of Labour History in London.

The original videotapes are held by the Television History Centre, together with copies of everything gathered during the project and our own photographs.

Although this is the end of the book, the process of recording the history of car making at Cowley is still continuing. We are working with the participants to collect more information and experience. If you would like to contribute to this history write to: Making Cars, 42 Queen Square, London WC1N 3AJ.

If you would like to compile and record the history of your place of work we have prepared a free pamphlet to help. The pamphlet offers suggestions and examples on how to go about recording your history. It is called Making History 1: The Factory.

If you would like to view the programmes, they are available on video together with a user pack of back-up materials.

The Television History Centre offers information help and advice, organises training days and can put you in touch with other groups. It produces a series of booklets to help people record their own history.

The History Workshop Sound and Video Archive, already contains hundreds of hours of sound and video recordings, catalogued and indexed for easy reference. It may have material you can use or you may wish to donate recordings to the Archive.

For more information about the Archive, the work of the Television History Centre or about other Television History Workshop programmes please write to

The Television History Centre,
  42 Queen Square,
    London,
      WC1N 3AJ

Participants

BB   Bill Buckingham, Morris Motors, Unipart 1938 to the present, TGWU

DB   Dave Buckle, Pressed Steel 1950–64, TGWU

EB   Ellen Bateman, Morris Motors 1915–21

JB   John Barr, Pressed Steel 1976 to the present, AUEW (Amalgamated Union of Engineering Workers)

NB   Norman Brown, Pressed Steel, Radiators 1935–47, AEU

PB   Peggy Burgess, Morris Motors 1940–5, ASTMS

TB   Tony Bradley, Morris Motors, Unipart 1939 to the present, AUEW

AC   Arthur Church, Pressed Steel 1935–75

LC   Leonard Coleman, Morris Motors 1979 to the present

RC   Rocky Claridge, Morris Motors 1951 to the present

LD   Len Dodds, Pressed Steel/ Morris Motors 1980 to the present

PD   Peter Davies, Pressed Steel 1960–80

AE   Arthur Exell, Morris Motors, Radiators 1929–75, AEU

HE   Haydn Evans, Pressed Steel 1933–74, TGWU (Transport and General Workers Union)/ ASTMS

HEC   Hugh Eccles, Manager, Unipart 1968–72

AF   Ada Fray, ex-tobacco worker

JF   John Fray, Pressed Steel 1959–75, AUEW

PF   Percy Fray, Pressed Steel 1927–69, TGWU

LG   Les Gurl, Morris Motors 1935–81, AEU

MG   Monty Gibbs, Morris Motors 1922–70

BH   Bill Honour, Pressed Steel 1926–69, TGWU/ASTMS

JH   John Hobbs, Pressed Steel 1940 to the present, TASS

MH   Monty Hillier, Morris Motors 1927–69

BJ   Bill Jupp, Pressed Steel 1952–80, TGWU

HJ   Hettie Jackson, Pressed Steel 1947–81

PJ   Peter Jarvis, Morris Motors 1972–80

RJ   Reginald Job, Designer, Morris Motors 1939–62

BK   Barry King, Pressed Steel 1971 to the present

CK   Colin Kilpatrick, Manager, Morris Motors 1966–81

HK   Harry Kerry, Morris Motors 1919–69

JK   Jenette King, Pressed Steel 1969–80

TK   Ted King, Line Operator, Pressed Steel 1947–80, TGWU

BL   Bill Lowe, Pressed Steel 1936–75

DL   Dave Lyddon, Pressed Steel 1972–7, TGWU

EL   Eric Lord, Manager and Managing Director, Morris Motors 1941–79

JL   John Lambourn, Pressed Steel/ Morris Motors 1956–63

RL   Richard Lee, Pressed Steel 1954–80

BM   Bob Moore, Manager, Morris Motors 1940–73

JM   Johnny Moxham, Pressed Steel 1940–81

KM   Kathy Moxham, Pressed Steel 1944–81, TGWU

TM   Tobi Mills, Morris Motors 1976 to the present

GP   George Price, Morris Motors 1924–66

JP   John Power, Shop Steward, Morris Motors/Unipart 1959–80, TGWU

MP   Max Parker, Pressed Steel 1939–70

PP   Pat Phipps, Morris Motors 1957 to the present, ASTMS

AR   Alec Robinson, Pressed Steel 1927–70, AUEW

BR   Bill Roche, Pressed Steel 1937 to the present, AUEW

TR   Tom Richardson, Morris Motors 1965–70

BS   Beverly Smith, Pressed Steel 1976–81

BSM Bill Smith, Pressed Steel 1975 to the present

ES   Enid Sims, Pressed Steel 1927–62

GS   Geoff Solomon, Pressed Steel 1947–78

HS   Harry Simpson, Morris Motors 1935–70

RS   Roger Sealey, Pressed Steel 1976 to the present, TGWU

SS   Sam Segaran, Morris Motors 1976 to the present

AT   Alan Thornett, Shop Steward, Pressed Steel 1959–82, TGWU

PT   Peter Tothill, BL Cars 1955–82

GW   George Weekes, Morris Motors 1924–71, AEU

TW   Tony Williamson, Shop Steward, Pressed Steel 1958 to the present, Lord Mayor of Oxford 1982/3

CY   Cyril Yeates, Morris Motors 1925–70, AEU

Acknowledgments and Photo Credits

Books

We acknowledge permission to quote from the following: *Autocar Magazine*, 1929; BL Heritage Catalogue; E. and F. Frow, *Engineering Struggles*, Working Class Movement Library, Manchester, 1982; R. J. Overy, *William Morris, Viscount Nuffield*, Europa Business Library, London, 1976; Peter Dunnett, *The Decline of the British Motor Industry*, Croom Helm, London, 1980; Pathé News.

Photographs

p.v   Car workers and assembly line, 1983 (Television History Centre (THC)/Webb)

p.5   Advert for BL Maestro made at Cowley, 1983 (BL Cars)

p.7   (*top*) Rural Oxford, *c.* 1900 (*Oxford Mail*)

p.7   (*left*) William Morris on his bike, 1908 (BL Heritage)

p.7   (*bottom*) Morris Motors takes over the military college at Cowley, 1918 (BL Heritage)

p.8   (*top*) Chassis drivers take a lunch break, *c.* 1925 (BL Heritage)

p.8   (*centre*) Harry Kerry, chassis driver, *c.* 1923 (THC/Kerry)

p.8   (*bottom*) Taking chassis for the engine and body to be added, *c.* 1923 (THC/Kerry)

p.11   Bodies finished using coach-building skills, *c.* 1920 (BL Heritage)

p.13   (*top*) Monty Gibb, centre, in his Bullnose Morris, *c.* 1926 (THC/Gibb)

p.13   (*bottom*) Massed cars show the scale of Morris production at Cowley, 1929 (BL Heritage)

p.15   (*top*) Trimshop women, 1926 (BL Heritage)

p.15   (*bottom*) Trimshop men, 1926 (BL Heritage)

p.19   (*top*) Morris Minor advertisement, 1929 (BL Heritage)

p.19   (*bottom*) Construction of Pressed Steel, 1926 (BL Heritage)

p.19   (*centre*) Letterhead, Pressed Steel, 1936 (THC)

p.25   (*bottom*) Leaving work at Cowley, 1929 (THC)

p.25   (*top*) Pressed Steel press, 1928 (BL Heritage)

p.31   Abe Lazarus, Communist Party industrial organiser, *c.* 1934 (THC/Exell)

p.37   (*top*) Pages from Alec Robinson's wage book, 1929–38 (THC)

p.36   (*centre*) George Mason's wedding, 1933 (THC/Wood)

p.36   (*bottom*) George Mason (centre) and friends, *c.* 1932 (THC/Wood)

p.48   (*top*) William Morris at Sports Day, 1934 (THC/Gibb)

p.48   (*centre*) Monty Hillier running at Oxford Sports Day *c.* 1948 (THC/Hillier)

128

p.48   (*bottom*) Morris Motors Band, 1930 (BL Heritage)

p.53   (*top left*) Women workers making mines, *c*. 1943 (BL Heritage)

p.53   (*top right*) Tanks at Cowley, 1944 (BL Heritage)

p.53   (*bottom right*) Woman welder, 1943 (BL Heritage)

p.55   Morris Motor Assembly, 1959 (BL Heritage)

p.63   Pickets at Cowley during the 1956 strike (*Oxford Mail*)

p.69   Piecework on the line, 1968 (BL Heritage)

p.87   Assembly line, 1966 (BL Heritage)

p.91   Assembly line, 1983 (THC/Webb)

p.95   (*top*) Women workers gauging parts, 1929 (BL Heritage)

p.95   (*bottom*) Trimworker, *c*. 1955 (BL Heritage)

p.99   Michael Edwardes and headline over extract from his book, 1984 (*Daily Mail*

p.109   (*bottom*) Assembly line, 1983 (THC/Webb)

p.128   History Shop, Cowley, and participants in programme, 1982 (THC/Webb)

Index

Broad subject areas are given in the Table of Contents. This index is for subjects and cross-references not otherwise readily apparent.